Wicked Waterbury

WICKED WATERBURY

MADMEN & MAYHEM IN THE BRASS CITY

EDITH REYNOLD
& JOHN MURRAY

THE
History
PRESS

Published by The History Press
Charleston, SC 29403
www.historypress.net

Copyright © 2009 by Edith Reynolds and John Murray
All rights reserved

First published 2009

Manufactured in the United States

ISBN 978.1.59629.629.9

Library of Congress Cataloging-in-Publication Data

Reynolds, Edith.
Wicked Waterbury : madmen and mayhem in the brass city / Edith Reynolds and John
Murray.
p. cm.
Includes bibliographical references.
ISBN 978-1-59629-629-9
1. Waterbury (Conn.)--History--Miscellanea. 2. Crime--Connecticut--Waterbury--History.
3. Violence--Connecticut--Waterbury--History. I. Murray, John, 1957- II. Title.
F104.W3R496 2009
974.6'8--dc22
2008048618

CONTENTS

contents

PREFACE

If headlines tell the story of a town, one might believe that crime has risen steadily from the 1850s. Newspapers in 1850 displayed a remarkable preponderance for temperance meetings, railroad timetables and occasionally news about events as mundane as rocks falling from a wall. Once in a while, an item appeared that seemed out of place, such as the day eleven-year-old Perry Upson was playing on the railroad track and was killed by a passing train.

The news was something you needed to know, whether it was to better your life or to watch for inherent danger—but there was not too much sensationalistic reporting. That is a far cry from the fear-driven newscasts of today, in which even the daily weather seems calamitous. It is no wonder, then, that there is almost no story too small to report today, and to catch the public's attention it has to contain a sensational element.

Victorians perceived their world as good. Ugly incidents and unfortunate circumstances happened, but they didn't necessarily want to read about it in their parlors. Bad things happened to the lower classes, and if they did happen to someone of means, then it was best left unsaid.

Perception today is something that Waterbury, like other cities, has to overcome. With a declining economic market during the last few decades, crime can be found almost anywhere. In Waterbury, however, it can be found in fewer places than most.

With populations maintaining a hundred thousand, some crime is expected. Even the Puritans had transgressors, despite their diligence in creating a God-fearing society eager to eliminate sin. But Waterbury stands out as a safe city, far safer than other towns equal in size.

We have our police department to thank for our safety in Waterbury, and we must also thank the neighborhoods, which are filled with caring and involved individuals. This wasn't always the case. This book stops at crimes committed or revealed up until the early 1980s. Where it ends, another series of crimes begins that could be contained in a whole separate volume.

At one point, after the second mayor and a local governor were sent to prison, citizens said, "Enough."

The current governance of the police, under the leadership of Chief Neal O'Leary, has worked to rid itself of poor practices and implemented model standards of community policing. With excellent response to emergencies, regular patrols and a plan for prevention, the citizens in this city reap many rewards. The implementation of a Police Activity League, which took over a closed elementary school and increased its membership to more than two thousand inner-city youths, has set a standard for caring about our children's futures.

Retired Deputy Chief Patrick Ridenhour, who is active in community affairs, cites the geographic nature of the city as a contributing factor for the safety. With neighborhoods often defined by hills, one neighborhood does not run into another as in Hartford or New Haven. Problems arising in one neighborhood are often contained until they can be solved. The geography also contributes to these several neighborhoods maintaining distinct characters filled with people who see their direct surroundings as a special place worth preserving.

That is why, whenever a horrific crime transpires, it is often shocking and unimaginable.

These good points don't necessarily mean that Waterburians don't grumble about the town. But it's much like a big family in which members can complain, but God help others who sling mud. Senatorial candidate Ned Lamont learned that lesson after the backlash from Waterbury voters who bitterly resented his campaign worker's remark that the town was "the crossroads of slime and evil."

Prior to the 1980s, when two mayors went to jail, people used to joke about corruption—the time between the Hayes trial and now was long enough to allow for poking fun. When Joe Lieberman ran for the Senate, he joked that if he died he would like to be buried in Waterbury so he could still vote. Mayor Bergin used to crack up poll workers with the statement that they were waiting for the results from St. Joe's Cemetery. After the city experienced scandal after scandal, the jokes stopped.

When the chips are down, Waterbury responds.

At the end of a troubled era of political corruption that gave the city a tarnished reputation far worse than T. Frank Hayes and his cronies instilled, a mayor was charged with the task of getting the city back on its feet and moving forward. When Mayor Michael Jarjura was defeated in a primary in 2005, citizens feared sliding back into a morass of poor governance and rallied a write-in vote that became national news.

Maybe it is the grit that the early settlers used to overcome the mucky roads and poor conditions to forge what would become a powerful city. The first one hundred years of this town were spent creating a community in the Naugatuck Valley. The second hundred years were ones of pure growth and prosperity. As in the first part of the city's history, everything was moving forward like a wave coming in toward shore. By the time of the tercentennial, Waterbury celebrated, but the forward movement had crashed and was on the ebb. Factories closed and were abandoned. People lost pensions that they had worked decades to earn. The infrastructure was getting old and was in need of repair.

Waterbury wasn't alone. The Northeast, which once was a swath of industry that fueled a booming economy, had now become a "rust belt." This book is not an account of that path, but it describes events as they happen throughout our city's history.

In researching the history of Waterbury crimes, I learned two things. The first is that what is considered a crime today may be considered normal behavior in the future. Waterbury's early settlers would publicly whip people who had intimate relations out of wedlock, even if they married afterward. In the 1930s, the focus was on birth control, and Waterbury was the battleground between concerned citizens who wanted women to be able to control the number of children they produced and those who felt that contraception was obscene and sinful. Today, young people are not publicly scourged, nor are clinics taken to court. Instead, healthcare and social service agencies work diligently to educate and provide good care and nurture families, no matter what the age or marital status of the parents.

The second thing I learned is that by reading news stories from decades past, one can see a shift in how information is presented. This can determine how one views things. The best example comes from two short news items from 1907.

John Cavanaugh appeared to be a typical police officer of his day— young, strong and athletic. He was a man who cared about his duty and the people he was sworn to protect. The first news report that year described how, while on duty at the train depot, Cavanaugh spotted a tiny, sixty-year-

Union Station was part of Officer Cavanaugh's beat. *Historical postcard, author's collection.*

old woman, hampered by an oversized and heavy valise, struggling to catch the Danbury train.

When the train pulled away without her, the woman burst into tears. Cavanaugh assured the woman that another train to Danbury would be along in an hour. The tears continued as she explained that her dying mother might not wait that hour.

Cavanaugh grabbed the woman and her valise and ran toward the departing train, calling for the conductor to stop. The conductor slowed the engine and stretched out to receive the woman, who Cavanaugh pushed into his arms before tossing the heavy bag onto the train.

From that story, we have a good idea of Cavanaugh's character. Some months later, he was patrolling the depot again. It was ten thirty on a Sunday morning and unseasonably cold. A shout called his attention toward the back of the Seery Street icehouse, where the Mahan Canal ran with ten feet of water and a heavy current. Five hundred feet away, a child had fallen into the water, and his two young companions were crying for help. Cavanaugh acted quickly and ran. He dove into the canal, still wearing his heavy woolen uniform and helmet. He rescued the child and brought him home to his parents on Sperry Street. Young Frank Laborda Jr. was sixteen months old, dripping wet and very happy to be home.

Cavanaugh returned to the police station, where he requested permission to go to his Hickory Street home to change his clothing before reporting back to work by noon.

The second story adds a few facts to our picture of Cavanaugh. Prior to joining the police force, he had worked at the local buckle factory and volunteered for the Phoenix Fire Company #1, where he distinguished himself by trying to save the life of Mrs. Mary Keefe, whose lamp had blown up. Cavanaugh wasn't successful, but not for want of trying. He had the badly burned hands to prove his determination.

How Cavanaugh's story was reported colored how readers viewed their city. This was a story about how lucky Waterbury was to have so noble a civil servant. Today, the sensationalism rampant in national media would have represented these facts in a far different manner. Cavanaugh would simply be a man doing his job. The headline would have touted how the Laborda family was under investigation by the Department of Children and Families (DCF) for allowing so young a toddler to play in a dangerous area improperly attended.

The year 1907 was a time of prosperity, and the city felt good about itself.

As times changed and the population became more diverse, factions began to occur. World War I was the point where perception changed. Worker unrest wasn't new, but the news from overseas was remarkable by any standard. A long, painful war introduced horrendous conditions and new ways for man to kill man. Governments were overthrown, and the peasants and working classes demanded control. Americans believed that we were beyond all that—that we had achieved a society of equality and prosperity.

Not everyone agreed. For many, there were severe problems relating to economic class differences, religious intolerance, racial prejudice and political strife. Waterbury, being a conservative city, viewed these changes as detrimental to a prosperous way of life. The city prided itself on rooting out Bolshevik sympathizers, as evidenced by the six Waterbury residents deported on the Soviet Ark. It also lauded its ability to prevent radical orator Carlo Tresca from gaining a toehold in the Brass City. Very few communities were able to brag about that.

But to some, the thoughts and changes that someone like Carlo Tresca might incite may have led to better working conditions. Perhaps a humanistic approach would have resulted in fewer victims of radium poisoning, people with severed limbs and worse.

Despite the control that the media exert in shaping our perceptions, the Fourth Estate is crucial to preserving our freedoms and rooting out crime.

Without the *Waterbury Republican-American*'s diligence, T. Frank Hayes might have bilked more millions from the coffers. Without the *Waterbury Observer*'s quests for justice, the Radium Girls' story might still be unheard.

A look at history is only part of the story. The first one hundred years here were spent creating a community from nothing. The second hundred were spent making it prosper. The third saw the pendulum swing higher before the fall, when industries abandoned environmentally unsafe factories and thousands of workers were left unemployed and pensionless. The city was left "holding the bag."

But as the city reemerged with a determination to create a safe home for its citizens, so, too, it was working to create a better future for its children.

John Murray owns and operates the *Waterbury Observer* and has made it his mission to bring more to the news than sensational facts. He also instigated this book and has provided me with invaluable insight. His reportage and publishing brings history to the Waterbury public every month for free. He is a true friend to this city.

I would like to thank my husband, Dan, for giving me the time away from the business of our bookstore and café to compile this book. Without the help from Lisa Bessette, Kristin DeFiore, Lance Gaston and Tom Palomba, our café staff, none of this would be possible. Special thanks goes to Vicky Semrow, whose constant technical assistance is never underrated and always appreciated.

Others helping with information were vital to constructing these chapters: Michael Dooling from the *Waterbury Republican-American* newspaper, Justin Donnelly, Lionel Alves, Maurice Mosely, Phil Benevento, Ken and Brenda Killer, the Silas Bronson Library, Ellyn and Bill Scully and Lieutenant Robert Maxwell and the Waterbury Police Department. I extend my thanks to all.

Edith Reynolds

CHAPTER 1

EARLY WAYS

Danger Beyond the Fence

Before the first white man traversed the Naugatuck Valley, woodland tribes staked out areas to hunt and live, following the food source and seasons in order to survive. The tribes throughout Connecticut were all Algonquins, but they were divided into smaller tribes of Pequots, Mohegans, Paugausetts, Quinnepiacs and the Tunxis. Each village was small, with ten to twelve dwellings housing up to one hundred people who lived communally. Waterbury was an area that remained untamed—because of the unpredictable nature of the Naugatuck River, the valley was useful for hunting but too unstable for settlement.

The first of the white settlers arrived in what was called Mattatuck in 1651, some eighty-six hundred years after the first native took up residence in New England. Minerals were the draw for the white men, but in 1657, when the area proved barren for mining, farmers drifted out of the Farmington plantation and settled on the western hilltop now called Town Plot. Initial relations with the natives were cordial, but they became strained when the Native Americans returned to hunt. Previous deeds that had been drawn up and signed by the tribal elders were nothing more than rental agreements since the tribe had no concept of owning land. The settlers made payment after payment, and this kindled a smoldering distrust. At the same time, the natives suffered greatly from European diseases like measles, which ran rampant through their camps, and they, too, began to rethink those cordial ties.

The first thirty families to settle the region chose the promontory now know as Town Plot, but before a true settlement of dwellings could be erected, the Indian war of New England broke out in 1675. The sachem Metacomet, also known as King Philip, led the war against white settlers. Attacks were launched in Deerfield, Providence and Simsbury, among other settlement villages. Men were needed for the fight, and the Town Plot families ran back to Farmington for safety. Seven out of eight Indians lost their lives in the conflict, and the population of settlers was decimated by half. In 1677, after the war ended, the returning settlers took another look at the landscape and determined that the lower meadows east of the river were more favorable for dwellings and pasture and closer to the safety of Farmington.

The decision could have been better. Heading south to Naugatuck or north to Watertown would have provided better farmland. Waterbury was a land of muck and flood. Paths set down for travel became swamps, and cattle would sink deep into the mud. Mosquitoes and other insects abounded, and the environment was rich for pestilence. But there was tenacity within this little community, and members set forth to plot out land and set up necessities like mills and a church.

The first proprietors were Puritans, and they kept the ideals that set them adrift from their native land of England. These brave souls moved first to Boston, then on toward Hartford and New Haven and then began to create smaller settlements throughout the Connecticut countryside. Waterbury was an offshoot of Farmington. With each settlement, the ideal community was envisioned, and laws and regulations were structured to prevent sin and to ensure the success of the community as a whole—perfect in God's eyes.

The first laws were practical. Deeds to properties, rights of inheritance, defense of the community and lawful marriages were necessary for a smooth-running society. Each member of the community was expected to work—idle hands were, after all, the devil's workshop. No one was rich or titled. This was a band of people with modest means who hoped to prosper by farming and through small, useful trades.

Each family had a responsibility to the community, which was ruled as a theocracy. Members were expected to sit on a grand council to decide laws and to regulate behavior. The first of those regulations was installing a protective fence around the settlement, with each family paying for a share and maintaining the structure. Failure to do so jeopardized the community at large, and undependable persons would be punished.

Prior to 1700, marriages were civil affairs performed by governors, assistants and commissioners. Baptisms took place right after birth. Wills

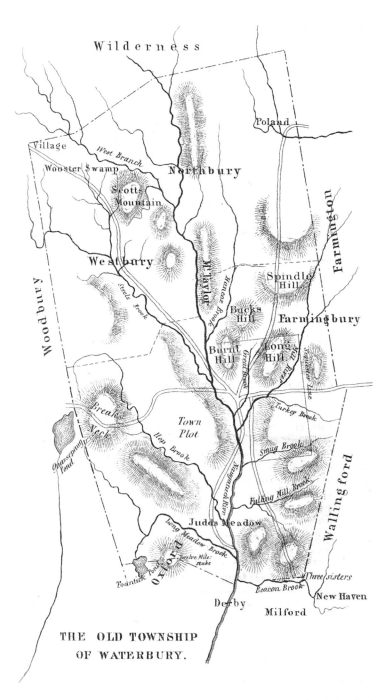

Waterbury was an offshoot of the Farmington colony, laid out along a flood plain in the style of English country towns. *Author's collection.*

and probate settled estates under a court of magistrates in a county system. Indolence and sexual transgressions were among the biggest hurdles to overcome in order to attain heavenly perfection. Puritans took that seriously.

Failure to attend church services on Sunday meant a fine of five shillings. If that fine was not paid, public whipping ensued. The use of tobacco in public brought a sixpence fine.

The son of James Olmstead was a wild youth; he was also married. In 1640, the young man was judged for moral delinquencies and was forced to pay a fine of twenty pounds and stand upon the pillory in Hartford.

Obadiah Richards was an early settler of Farmington and was made a freeman in 1669. He became active in the Mattatuck enterprise as one of the first settlers. He was one of the Town Plot pioneers before the final move to the valley below. As a proprietor, he had a share in the division of the common fence, but when a crisis arose it was discovered that Obadiah had not obeyed the articles of law overseeing the management of the fence. He was deemed tardy and had a slipshod way of doing things, according to Dr. Henry Bronson in the first *History of Waterbury*.

Obadiah's allotments were condemned in 1682–83, and in order to restore his rights in the community he had to overcome his defects. Other than laziness, he was considered an excellent man. But the community at large had to be able to depend upon each individual to be responsible for the community welfare.

One must remember that these settlers faced great hardship. It wasn't as if they moseyed off to some campground and set up a village. These people immersed themselves amidst a community of people quite unlike themselves, people who were increasingly disenchanted with the settlers' presence. Following King Philip's War, the remaining natives held grudges over the slaughter of their warriors and the enslavement of women and children.

Outside the communal fence lurked serious danger. Settlers venturing beyond the fields alone were at great risk. Intermittent incidents reinforced their fears. One itinerant traveler named Holt was ambushed in what is now Plymouth—a rumor was spread that his tongue had been removed.

The Indians mastered the art of stalking, sneaking up on their prey and taking captives by surprise. Torture and mutilation sometimes ensued. Their ferocity and audacity were fanned by an alliance with the French in Canada. The French had a direct conflict going with England over land ownership, and using the Indians saved on the cost of equipping and using French soldiers. Settlements (like Deerfield) were burned, and captives were taken north and held for ransom—that is, if they lived. Some captives chose to remain with their captors.

In 1710, Indians moved in from the west and surprised a father and two sons who were lunching beneath a tree. While Jonathan Scott fought the attacking Indians, the boys ran for help. The Indians quickly overcame the man and told him that they would spare his life and the farm if he recalled the boys. The boys returned to save their father, but not before Scott's captors cut off his thumb to cripple him, preventing him from escaping.

The family was taken, leaving wife and mother Hannah Hawkes Scott alone to live with her father. Theirs was a family used to the bedevilment of Indians. While living in Deerfield, Hannah's mother, her brother John, his wife and three children were massacred. A sister, Elizabeth, was captured, but she died en route to Canada.

The community provided what it could to help Hannah and her father, scraping together the ransom money for release. In 1711, Jonathan and his eldest son returned; the younger boy chose to remain behind.

According to Henry Bronson, the typical Indian was not the noble savage some might think. The general character, as far as Puritans were concerned, included lying, cheating, thieving, laziness, thriftlessness, a lack of faith and bloodthirsty leanings. Drunkenness was one vice, Bronson said, that the Indian inherited from contact with white men, and when drunk, the Indian lapsed into a state quite like a wild animal.

The case of Moses Paul is a good example of what led to this belief. Moses Paul was a Brotherton Indian, an offshoot of the Pequot tribe. While in Bethany in 1771, Waterburian Moses Clark was killed during a drunken argument. Clark was not Paul's intended target, but the Indian's inebriation caused him to swing and miss, landing a fatal blow on the unsuspecting Clark. Paul was sentenced to hang and had asked an Indian preacher named Samsom Occum to speak at the execution. The sermon against drunkenness was a cornerstone in establishing a temperance movement.

Waterbury was a community that worked hard all day and spent the nights watching for danger. Every man was trained in defense; every settlement maintained a militia. Military ranks were awarded, thereby creating a hierarchy within the small, poor communities. At the turn of the eighteenth century, Waterbury was a community of about two hundred, broken up into thirty to thirty-five families.

Another facet of Puritan life was witchcraft. Most people are familiar with the Salem witch trials in Massachusetts, but Connecticut was rife with witches—if the arrest roles are to be believed.

A

SERMON

PREACHED

AT THE

EXECUTION OF

MOSES PAUL,

AN INDIAN,

Who was executed at New-Haven, on the 2d of

September 1772.

FOR THE

MURDER OF

MR. MOSES COOK,

Late of Waterbury, on the 7th of December 1771.

Preached at the desire of said Paul.

BY SAMSON OCCOM,
Minister of the gospel, and missionary to the Indians.

SPRINGFIELD.

HENRY BREWER—PRINTER.

The sermon by Samson Occum, an Indian preacher, delivered at the execution of Moses Paul, was distributed and became the cornerstone of the temperance movement. *Author's collection.*

Witchcraft was a capital crime in a theocracy. Satan was unwelcome in the Puritan settlements, and any invitations brought danger to the entire community. The Puritans believed that they had enough to contend with without adding Old Scratch into the mix.

Witch trials contained more than a simple accusation. In practice, there had to be some damage that would account for a legal proceeding. For those women accused and acquitted, suits for slander also made their way into the courts. Until 1662, only one witness or complainant was needed to make an accusation. Following that year, it required multiple testimonies.

According to state records, the first trial began in 1647 and ended in hanging. From that time to 1697, forty-five people (both men and women) were tried. Five were hanged and three were probably executed. Some fled the state, but most were acquitted. Waterbury was missing from the roles, testifying to both the rigors with which this community policed its inhabitants and the seriousness with which the community approached its values.

As a new century dawned, the small hamlet of Waterbury began to see new faces blend into the fabric of their community. Settlers in the New World were no longer just religious pioneers, but also English who wanted to create better lives for themselves.

It was an expanding colony, and with the native problems removed to the west or assimilated into Connecticut towns, settlers could focus on more mercantile concerns that built small settlements into more prosperous towns. Of course, with prosperity comes taxation, and England wanted more and more of its due.

People in Waterbury lived, died and broke the law. Bronson lists the transgressions found during the eighteenth century.

One couple from Bucks Hill married in April 1736 and gave birth to their firstborn the following September. Because it was clear that they had engaged in premarital sex, the couple was summoned to Hartford, where the penalty was five pounds or ten stripes (probably apiece).

Miles Wooster and Samuel Sprerry were each fined three shillings apiece for profane behavior between meetings on the Sabbath.

In 1761, Isaac Frazier broke into the shop of Joseph Hopkins to steal more than a hundred pounds worth of goldsmith work. When sentenced to execution, he begged the court to commute the sentence to imprisonment, banishment or slavery. The court did not comply.

Hardship placed on families often led to desperate measures. In 1783, Peter Gilkey was found to possess counterfeiting tools. He was sent to Newgate Prison and his estate forfeited. Gilkey threw himself on the court's mercy, explaining that he had a lame hand and his family was destitute. He fully intended to break the law, he admitted, but had not done so. He was released from prison.

His friend Isaac Hine was also arrested but acquitted.

Economic times weren't much better in 1785, when John Porter and Elnathan Jennings were charged with counterfeiting coins. Rather than throw themselves on the mercy of the court, as Gilkey had done, the pair escaped twice and were recaptured, making a clean getaway the third time.

Revolution Introduced the Crime of Treason

The centerpiece of history within the eighteenth century was the American Revolution. The fervor that led up to the Continental Congress grew over decades of what the settlers believed to be England's systematic bleeding of the colony's economic resources. After struggling with the hardships of carving out a new land, the settlers wanted the opportunity to grow and prosper.

Sentiment for both sides ran high in communities along the eastern seaboard. Waterbury was no exception. The calls for loyalty and revolution pealed in every household, and it was time to make a stand. This sometimes meant that families sitting around the dinner table were becoming sworn enemies. In the case of Moses Dunbar, the fervor reached its peak. Moses, a Loyalist husband and father of seven, bucked his father's revolutionary politics and went to work for the English as an army captain, recruiting soldiers for General Howe and his army.

Moses wasn't alone in his Tory leanings, but it wasn't a popular stance. He recounts in his biography that at one point he was attacked by a band of forty men. After moving to Long Island, Dunbar made a trip home and, while there, was betrayed by a neighbor, Joseph Smith. The Waterbury authorities refused to push the matter forward and sent Dunbar to justice in Farmington. He was removed by the court to Hartford, where he was judged on January 23, 1777. He was to be executed the following March near where Trinity College now stands.

In March of that year, a close friend and Loyalist supporter, Elisha Wadsworth, brought Dunbar a secreted knife with which the prisoner was able to undo his chains. He knocked down the guards before fleeing. Dunbar was recaptured (along with Wadsworth, who was tried and fined forty pounds), sentenced to a year in prison and fined the cost of prosecution.

Moses Dunbar has the distinction of being the only Loyalist hanged in Connecticut.

Prior to the execution, and despite the severity of his son's sentence, the elder Dunbar offered no condolence; rather, he offered Connecticut the hemp to be used for the noose.

The Reverend Mr. Nichols of Waterbury was similarly tried but acquitted.

In this case, too, the elder Dunbar was a staunch supporter of the Revolution, a situation that was mirrored in so illustrious a family as the Franklins. While Benjamin was seated at the Continental Congress, his son William was the last Tory governor of New Jersey.

William Franklin was imprisoned in Connecticut and, along with other Tory prisoners, found the conditions so harsh that he harbored ill feeling toward the new country long after the end of the war.

Given the history and conditions of Newgate Prison, it was easy to see why the prisoners' rancor didn't subside. Located in East Granby, the prison formerly served as a copper mine, maybe the first in Connecticut. It opened for incarceration in 1773 to house a burglar. During the Revolution, it was used as a jail for Tory prisoners.

Reassimilation after the war was difficult for former Loyalists, who chose to retreat to a life in Canada rather than endure the difficulties at home. In the case of Reverend James Scovill and his son, they parted over separate loyalties. After living sixty years in New Brunswick, the younger Scovill refused to ever return to his hometown.

Others who returned after the Revolution ended recanted their political leanings and built a life in Waterbury. It wasn't until 1784 that former Tories were allowed to participate in politics, but after that time they counted for one-third of the voting population.

CHAPTER 2

WHAT WE DO FOR LOVE

Victorian Love Triangle

The turmoil of an emerging nation was the impetus to the development of the brass industry in the Naugatuck Valley. One of the most famous legends of Waterbury is that brass workers were smuggled out of England in barrels and brought to Waterbury. Glamorous as it may seem, it simply isn't true.

But brass did come to the community in the nineteenth century, and the growth of enterprise allowed for the community to thrive and then become a leader in the Industrial Revolution.

People flooded into town to work, and when the existing Americans filled the factories, new blood was drawn from the shores of Europe. Italians, French, Portuguese, Irish and others began to settle in one neighborhood or another. With them came new customs. Here they made money and lived well.

Crime and politics seemed to go hand in hand in Waterbury. That legacy began in 1883, when Mayor Greene Kendrick was the first politician involved in a public scandal. At noon on April 17, busy pedestrians downtown heard screams of "murder!" According to the newspaper account of the day, one hundred people rushed to an apartment door and found a man blocking his eyes and thrashing around in a panic. Mrs. Sarah Clark explained that she had blinded her husband William with red pepper after he tried to break into her bedroom. A blow to the head instantly quelled the husband's lack of chivalry, and the police whisked the hapless mechanic off to the station house.

Mayor Greene Kendrick's pleasant drives with another man's wife were scandalous behavior for Victorian times. Waterbury Observer *Archives, John Murray.*

Clark demanded to see the mayor immediately. The mayor refused, saying that he would not interrupt his lunch.

But when William threatened dire political consequences for the mayor if he did not respond, Kendrick finally appeared. After a moment of whispering in a corner between the mayor and the bleeding man, the incident was dropped without charges. The mechanic was released into the mayor's custody. It seems that Kendrick didn't want the quiet lunches in New Haven and the pleasant country drives he had taken with Clark's wife made public.

Hanging Bessie Wakefield

Love scandal wasn't resigned to the mayoral class in Waterbury. A few decades later, in 1913, a murder involving a Waterbury man, James Plew, generated a great deal of publicity.

This was the Bessie Wakefield trial, in which it was charged that Bessie and her lover, James Plew, conspired and killed Bessie's husband, William, in Bristol, Connecticut. According to the news reports of the day, the body was found dumped in a patch of woods in nearby Cheshire.

Bessie quickly confessed to police, claiming that it had been a plot hatched between lovers. According to Bessie, her husband was an abusive man, and this strain upon their marriage led her to the arms of Waterburian James Plew.

The Wakefields moved to Bristol from Middlebury. The couple had been separated because of William's jealousy over the attentions Plew paid to his wife. The move to another city was their attempt at reconciliation, but Bessie's account stated that a week before William's body was found, Plew arrived at their new home. It was then that the couple decided to be rid of Wakefield, and to that end, Bessie left the men alone, suggesting to Plew that her husband be pushed into a nearby lake.

According to what she claimed that Plew told her, the men quarreled. Plew choked William and chloroformed him into senselessness. With the victim in that state, Plew led William through the countryside of Bristol and Southington, on foot, for ten miles until he reached a heavily wooded portion of Cheshire. William's body was found five hundred feet from the highway.

Plew admitted that he had shot and stabbed Bessie's husband. One last touch was added. Plew took the dead man's shoelaces and tied them first around the victim's neck and then to a tree in order to make the death look like a suicide.

Plew then returned to Bristol, and Bessie reported her husband's disappearance to the police, stating that she was afraid he'd harm himself.

The coroner ruled that the cause of death was two shots to the back of the head and a stab wound to the heart. Bessie was apprehended immediately. Plew was later arrested in Middlebury, and the pair was taken to Waterbury before transport to the New Haven jail.

Waterbury attorney Thomas P. Devine represented Plew in court in front of Judge Burpee of New Haven. The pair was found guilty, and Burpee sentenced both to hang for their crimes.

Plew went to the gallows.

Bessie made it into the newspapers when suffragists took up her cause, citing spousal abuse, as well as the influence of a sinful man, as a mitigating factor. Bessie, if the sentence stood, would have been the first woman executed in the state since the Connecticut witch trials of 1647–53. A total of fifteen hundred appeals flooded the office of Governor Baldwin, and thousands more signed petitions that urged the state to reconsider the sentence.

Letters to the editors expressed differing viewpoints. Some demanded that Bessie be held accountable for her crime. She had chosen and knew full well that her husband would be killed, leaving her child fatherless.

Baldwin commuted the sentence in 1914.

South End Shootout

Waterbury headlines leading up to the Christmas season of 1919 read: "Men Battle to Death in Pistol Duel Over Woman on Benedict St." and "Fusillade of Bullets Fired with Lightning Rapidity into Body of Peter Cecera by Joseph Catardo."

Alleged white slaver Catardo gunned down Cecera in a small diner during an argument over a woman and money. The heated exchange ended when both men pulled out six-shooters and began firing at each other. A New Haven sailor, Howard Lawlor, witnessed the event and explained to police that Catardo's friend's "common law wife" was seriously ill in New Britain. She owed Catardo a small debt, which he wanted to collect upon his return from a trip to Italy. The woman was to pay him from the money owed to her by Cecera. Cecera, a Crown Street resident, was known by the police as a pimp who reneged on debts.

Little sympathy was forthcoming for Peter Cecera. The consensus of the Italian residents in Cecera's neighborhood, according to the newspaper, was that he'd gotten what he deserved.

Barlow and the Poison Needle

On another echelon of Waterbury society, on November 7, 1919, a novelties manufacturer in Waterbury named Erastus Barlow was in Richmond, Virginia, meeting with attorney Harry Grace, the nephew of a woman Barlow was suing for breach of promise.

The woman in question was Courtney Lindsay, who was separated from her husband and who had corresponded and become intimate with Barlow for three years. The breach came when Mrs. Lindsay found another beau, Dr. John A. Marr, who owned and operated a sanitarium for the inebriated in Richmond.

Barlow was explaining himself, while his niece Mildred Curtis acted as secretary. She soon turned into a witness and hero when Dr. Marr suddenly burst out from behind a door and wrestled with Barlow before jabbing the novelties manufacturer's hand with a needle.

Barlow forced the doctor to retreat by pretending to have a concealed weapon.

The respite from the attack allowed Curtis to rush her uncle out of danger and into the hands of a physician, who attested that the syringe contained poison.

The case went to court.

The judge in Richmond, where the case was heard, fined each man and ordered both to keep the peace for a year.

CHAPTER 3

CHANGING TIMES

Death by Trolley

Trolleys, or trams as they are sometimes called, were introduced during the latter half of the nineteenth century. Waterbury, like many other major cities, utilized the service and installed a system that transported people into the heart of the city on a daily basis.

Trolleys weren't foolproof, and they posed as much danger as gas-powered transportation does today. In addition, there was a long overlap of automated vehicles with the traditional horse-drawn conveyances, and that sometimes proved fatal.

In 1907, this was the case. That year, in Chattanooga, Tennessee, four were killed and twenty injured, with half of those being hospitalized due to a head-on collision between two trolleys. Two of the four killed were motormen. The cause was a broken signal.

In Stamford, Connecticut, the Myrtle Avenue line was operating on a cold October night. The cold rails caused the trolley brakes to fail, and as passengers locked into the car quaked with fright, the car sped alongside a river before overturning.

In Waterbury, poor Raffele De Marco was killed when a trolley collided with the horse-drawn concrete wagon he was driving. The thirty-four-year-old man had been hauling concrete mix for his employer, J.D. Barbara Concrete and Masonry. De Marco's wagon was struck at the corner of Grand Street and South Main, only one block from his Canal Street home. The trolley, said some witnesses, was traveling at a high rate of speed when

Trolley car safety was a major concern for passengers. This November 1907 accident shows a trolley after being hit and dragged by a locomotive. Twenty-nine passengers were onboard. *Photo postcard, author's collection.*

Trolleys are seen at Exchange Place, one block away from the accident that claimed the life of Raffele De Marco. *Postcard, author's collection.*

it smashed into the wagon, throwing De Marco back onto the bed. The trolley failed to stop and hit the wagon once more, tossing De Marco onto the street, where his head was crushed beneath the wheels.

Medical examiner A.A. Crane and Deputy Coroner W.D. Makepeace responded immediately to the gruesome scene and declared that De Marco's broken neck was the immediate cause of death but the crew was at fault. Patrolman Joseph Nagle arrested motorman James Sullivan of Naugatuck and conductor Sylvester Hoyt.

Arresting a trolley engineer and conductor for manslaughter was highly unusual. Serious accidents that resulted in death and a major trolley strike did foster a feeling of resentment among some. The conductor in the photo is unknown. *Author's collection.*

According to Ellyn Bergin Scully, De Marco was taken to Bergin Funeral Home, where the funeral parlor's records listed his cause of death as manslaughter.

Sullivan was held on a $5,000 bond and Hoyt on $2,000.

A few days later, Sullivan's attorney petitioned the court and was granted a reduction of bond to $2,000, whereupon Makepeace threatened to rearrest the motorman should he try to leave jail. Police Superintendent George M. Beach concurred.

Other tragic trolley incidents include George Leonard, who, at 12:15 a.m., stumbled onto the tracks, where his legs and feet were crushed, and the triple deaths of World War I veteran Antonio Becce, age twenty-nine; Antonio's son, Pasquale Becce, age two; and Vito Lavagno, age twenty-four. The triple death occurred at Lakewood when an automobile spooked the horse drawing Becce's carriage. The horse reared and backed the carriage into a guardrail, which gave way under the weight. When the rail broke, the three passengers dropped into the lake and drowned. The families sued the city.

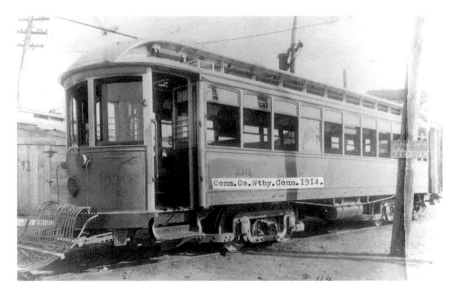

This 1914 trolley car shows that it was little more than a box filled with seats riding on wheels. It was, however, an essential form of public transportation. *Photo postcard, author's collection.*

Wobblies in Waterbury

The beginning of the twentieth century was a time of great growth and prosperity for the United States, and Waterbury was not left behind. Business was king, but it was also a time of change. There was a growing demand in factories for eight-hour days, some time off and fair wages. As a result, union strife brought lawlessness into a new realm and muddied the waters of what would be considered right and wrong.

A new movement for unions was the general union. The general union was set up for political change, as opposed to trade unions, which oversaw a particular set of skilled workers. The brass industry workers fell into the metal working unions, but the Industrial Workers of the World (IWW, or Wobblies as its members came to be known) wanted to create a widespread political base and hoped to absorb Waterbury workers into its fold.

Trolley conductors were among the American workers who went on strike, a move the public criticized. Waterbury did not want to see any more strikes and worked diligently to prevent the powerful IWW from gaining a foothold in town. *Author's collection.*

The first targets of the Wobblies, however, weren't workers of the Naugatuck Valley. They built their numbers with unaffiliated workers like lumberjacks and laborers. Gaining a strong base of agrarian and unskilled workers, the next targets were the members of more established unions, and Waterbury was one of the cities that the Wobblies hoped to poach.

The tactics used by the IWW and the response by industry to the threats were extreme by today's standards. Wobblies liked to show their strength by creating fear in the ruling class, while demonstrating the power of united workers. General strikes brought business and daily life to a standstill. Bombs were sent through the mail to wreak terror in communities. Industrial sabotage was implemented.

This launched a debate on both sides. Middle- and upper-class Americans wanted to preserve safety without losing the right to free speech. Anarchists fought amongst themselves over the ideology to follow. Some factions preferred socialism; others recommended fascism.

Waterbury was not left out of the fray. In 1904, a general tram strike turned violent, resulting in deaths. Bitter feelings lingered, and when a moving trolley killed a man in 1907, the trolley personnel were charged with manslaughter.

Workers toiled under harsh factory conditions. The brass industry wasn't a genteel trade, but rather one that involved long hours and stamina. With World War I demanding munitions, the brass barons demanded that the need be met. Grumblings began among the immigrant workers, who were fed by the successes fascism and socialism were gaining in their homelands.

This city was intent on keeping Wobblies out and capitalism flourishing. The ruling class in town saw no problem with what capitalism accomplished. The change from poor farms to thriving business was the result of capitalism. Wasn't Waterbury now the Brass Capital of the World?

This was no exaggeration. By 1895, there were eighteen brass mills in the United States, with six located in Waterbury and others scattered throughout the Naugatuck Valley. Over ten thousand workers were employed in Waterbury by those factories. Connecticut accounted for 75 percent of products coming from brass-rolling mills, a third of all brass castings and half of all brassware produced.

The reason behind the growth came from the city's most prevalent resource—water. The same water that mired the wheels on carts, sucked cattle hooves deep, caused floods and allowed pestilence to thrive was the resource that ensured the success of the brass industry. Water was the first power source for fledgling factories, but it later became the staple for annealing and washing metal.

The brass industry began in Waterbury, earning it the nickname the Brass City. For more than a century, it provided jobs. The never-ending need for brass led to a steady influx of immigrant labor. *Author's collection.*

It was the prosperity brass brought that built a remarkable water system, laid gas and electric lines, produced a bustling train terminal, established progressive schools and provided neighborhoods filled with gracious homes.

Against this backdrop, industries suffered from worker unrest. Things festered until World War I caused the IWW to take a strong stand for American pacifism. The Wobblies hoped that, with America allowing Europe to fight for itself, it would vanquish the class system, and peasants and workers would be allowed to rule their own countries.

When America began to supply goods to the war effort, the lumber industry received a hit. Spikes were hammered into spruce trees slated for use in airplane construction, rendering the wood useless. Transportation and defense workers, likewise, took a stand for neutrality. Meanwhile, Waterbury was pumping out artillery casings and machine and ship parts for the war.

Extraordinary measures were put into place by the United States government. The Sedition and Espionage Acts were enforced to keep the country safe, and anarchy was seen as a "Red Threat." It was during this period that Russia overthrew the tsar and established a socialist/communist regime. This spurred workers to greater heights of confidence that such change could happen here, with those who produced wealth in charge of distributing that wealth more fairly.

A new attorney general was named. A. Mitchell Palmer of Pennsylvania was a liberal who inherited a big problem. This former supporter of women's suffrage and workers' rights was faced with thirty-eight bombs sent through the U.S. postal system. One bomb exploded outside Palmer's home, killing the anarchist sent to deliver it.

Teaming up with a young attorney named J. Edgar Hoover, Palmer used the Sedition and Espionage Acts to launch a counterattack. Beginning on November 7, 1919, the first of what would become known as the Palmer Raids began. The date was the second anniversary of the Russian Revolution, so Palmer's message was clear about what and whom he wanted to stop. Knowing this would be a day when workers gathered, he ordered troops and police to round up as many union activists as they could find. Once apprehended, the alleged criminals were put in detention without being charged and held for a long period. Among those caught up in Palmer's dragnet were six Waterbury workers.

Officers Con Kiersted and Tim Hickey sit inside one of Waterbury's early vehicles. During the Palmer raid in town, police picked up dozens of alleged conspirators. *Postcard, author's collection.*

Federal agents from the Department of Justice and Secret Service came into the Naugatuck Valley in Ansonia and Waterbury to muster the police for the raid. Those targeted were radicals already under local police surveillance.

That night, the entire Waterbury police force reported for duty. Officers approached the raid with vigor but met no resistance. Fifty-three were arrested in the sweep and charged with spreading Bolshevism. At the station, police reported that the prisoners were given the "third degree."

Awaiting interrogation, the group huddled and sang the "Star-Spangled Banner" and "La Marseillaise" (the French national anthem).

Ansonia's dragnet arrested twenty-seven suspected Bolsheviks.

Six of those arrested in Waterbury received a stiff sentence—deportation. Those men were Joseph Keanesis, Lithuanian, from Wilson Street; John Borgnis, Italian, from Naugatuck; John Bokas, Lithuanian, from Riverside Street; Broney Leedake, Lithuanian, from Thomaston; George Wolkoff, Russian; and Zeno Bogen, Russian, from Crown Street.

A transatlantic ship named the *Buford* was commissioned to transport the seditious aliens from America to Finland. Dubbed the "Soviet Ark," the ship held two hundred passengers, among them the notable Emma Goldman. It was hoped that the prisoners would find their way to a country more hospitable to their political leanings, like the Soviet Union.

Palmer approved more raids across the United States in January 1920, using local law enforcement bolstered by troops. His excuse for the massive roundups was that agents received a tip that workers were planning to overthrow the government on May Day, the socialist Labor Day. Palmer contended that workers meeting that day to celebrate would start a process of anarchy.

The date came and went without incident, leading critics to be suspicious of the attorney general's motives. They suspected that the plot was a ruse to gain support for his candidacy for president.

The public was confused. A growing number of factory workers saw value in the socialist movement. They wanted to see improvement in their lives, not endless drudgery. The government raids were viewed as curtailing free speech in direct violation of the country's Constitution. Other citizens were simply fearful of having their lives disrupted.

Everyone in Waterbury watched the Wobblies' progress with interest.

The interest wasn't unfounded. Changes were being made elsewhere. In North Dakota, workers voted in a state assembly with a nonpartisan league that wanted to implement state-owned grain silos to benefit farm workers. This political upset demonstrated the power of what 200,000 union workers in thirteen states could accomplish at the polls.

Following World War I, there was continued unrest. Europeans felt that the Allied promises had failed to come to fruition. A flu epidemic decimated families, who were faced with staggering inflation, widespread unemployment and a lack of security. When the war ended, nine million defense workers and four million soldiers were out of work and faced an uncertain future. Socialism and fascism promised better times.

In 1919, thirty-six hundred strikes were called, and inflation nearly doubled food prices, as well as increased the cost of furniture and clothing. People were unhappy.

In January, a general strike of shipyard workers in Seattle crippled the city. Other strikes targeted garbage collection, laundry services, milk delivery, coal and water. A mix of fifteen hundred police officers and fifteen hundred government troops was called in to quell the unrest.

J. Edgar Hoover was tagged to form what would become the Federal Bureau of Investigation, and the newly formed group got to flex its muscles at the next big strike. It happened in Boston when police officers went on strike and crime soared. Riots and looting frightened the public until the National Guard moved in and implemented a curfew. Rioters were forced back by machine guns.

The Waterbury brass manufacturers watched fellow industrialists suffer. Steelworkers walked off the job in order to obtain the eight-hour day and wages above poverty level. No one wanted to work twelve-hour shifts seven days a week anymore.

The biggest headlines came when 394,000 coal workers walked off the job. The American public needed coal for heat, and wartime measures were put into effect. No one returned to work until Woodrow Wilson negotiated a settlement.

On Armistice Day, a massacre occurred in Centralia, Washington. Parading veterans joined citizens to raid the local union hall, where workers were assembled. A gunfight broke out, with shots fired from both sides. Several people were killed.

One of the union workers was Wesley Everest, who tried to escape. He was captured and incarcerated. Jailers later turned him over to a lynch mob. Their wrath and fear was made manifest in their actions. Members of the mob broke Everest's teeth with a gun butt, castrated him and lynched him four times in four different locations before riddling his dead body with bullets.

The coroner's finding was that the escaped prisoner, Wesley Everest, tied a noose around his neck and jumped from a bridge while shooting himself full of holes.

Closer to home, a New York house was raided, and agents found a hidden room containing enough explosives to make a hundred bombs.

As in Puritan times, the fray stayed pretty much outside Waterbury's "fence."

An oral history taken of artist Michele Russo by Jane Van Cleve in 1983 allowed the painter to reconstruct his impressions of his Waterbury childhood. He remembered that his family came from Italy to find work, and his father obtained employment at a local clock factory. He supported his stay-at-home wife, three daughters and Michele. Later, the semiliterate Nick Russo studied English and became an insurance agent, eventually opening his own firm.

During a visit to Italy with his mother and sisters, World War I broke out and the family was detained in Europe until 1919. Michele was ten when they returned to America, and he had to relearn English while attending grammar school.

He recalled that it was a progressive school, and the student body was made up of immigrant children whose parents worked in local industry. Teachers at both the grammar school level and in high school were encouraging. Michele remembered a number of amenities to the curriculum, like a pool, shop classes and even cooking and lunch programs. The high school boasted twenty-three Latin teachers.

Russo gained entry to Yale University to study art, a financial hardship on the family, but one it gladly bore for the sake of obtaining a good education for their only son.

About political matters, Michele stated:

The immigrant groups from my community were, I would say, carriers of radicalism. They were anarchists and they were other people, socialists of all kinds and atheists, particularly. It seems that all the male members of the ghetto community were atheists, in that religion was relegated to the women and the children. There was a great deal of political discussion and activity and a strong feeling of working class. Working-class philosophies were highly discussed. As a child I remember the Sacco/Vanzetti cases, the activities of the anarchists who organized the unions. I remember Carlo Tresca making frequent trips to Connecticut and working-class movements.

I remember also that out of this atmosphere there was a very strong anti-Fascist movement in the early days, which eventually was crushed by the fact that Fascism in Italy became the ruling regime of the Italian people, so that most of the Italians in the community eventually were brought into line with supporting Mussolini. Though I think the people from my particular community remained anti-Fascist all through that period of time to the last. This is indicative of the kind of environment I was brought up in. There was a great deal of discussion and I was very much aware of the discussion.

Lionel Alves of Watertown remembers his grandparents' connection to activist Carlo Tresca. "My grandparents had a boardinghouse in Stafford Springs, Connecticut, that catered to anarchists." Being a leftist, Luigi Remor struck up a friendship with Tresca, though, according to Alves's Aunt Nina, "Nonna didn't like him very much."

Alves, a Yale graduate, said the socialist leanings during that period grew out of poor wage compensation and trade unions without much power. The IWW was promising a society where workers controlled the flow of products and shared in the compensation.

Both fascism and Nazi ideologies had a socialist component, building on this post–World War I movement. Tresca adhered to a syndicalist theory that was more egalitarian in its views. It put Mussolini at odds with Tresca, the son of a wealthy landowner who had edited leftist newspapers in both Italy and the United States. The rift was so deep that when Tresca was assassinated in 1943, after eluding government agents who were following him, it was thought that it was a Mafia hit ordered by Il Duce.

But in March 1923, Tresca was a long way from his untimely death and standing on the doorstep of Waterbury. Two thousand people of Italian descent came to hear him speak at the Concordia Building on Bank Street. Tresca never got the chance to utter a single word from the Connecticut Constitution's Declaration of Rights, which he had planned to read aloud. Police Superintendent George M. Beach ordered police officers to the stage to remove the labor agitator. Deputy Superintendent McLean led the charge.

Tresca's lawyer, Charles Bauby, stated that the Italians who had come to hear Tresca speak were infuriated. Fascists had been employed by the police to heckle the speakers and disrupt the quiet gathering. He claimed to have seen officers poking the "plants" with nightsticks, urging them to start something.

Presiding onstage with the speaker were former Governor Baldwin's grandson Roger of Middlebury, the Reverend Frederick Laudenburn of Middletown and Rabbi Lewis Browne of Temple Israel in Waterbury. All three were members of the American Civil Liberties Union. Also on hand were attorney A. Henry Weisman and two brothers by the name of De Cicco.

Inside the hall, nearly ninety police officers and detectives were on hand, frisking everyone who entered, including Tresca. Two men from New Haven were immediately arrested, one for carrying a knife and the other for having a loaded pistol. Four federal officers from the Department of Justice were also present.

Tresca dined that night at a small dinner party on Meadow Street, vowing to return to Waterbury to speak publicly and to file suit against the police for harassment.

While Tresca dined on Meadow Street, another dinner party was being held at the Italian Republican Club, with Armando and Gennaro Pelosi presiding. It was a celebratory gathering to give thanks that the likes of Tresca would not be allowed to speak in Waterbury. Superintendent Beach received cheers for his part in breaking up the crowd. Michael Orione added his condemnation of the gathering, citing that it was ironic that a Christian minister and a Jewish rabbi would back the likes of a self-avowed atheist like Tresca.

During the religious services on March 17, Rabbi Browne issued a statement to members of his temple. He defended his participation in the Tresca affair. Freedom of speech as a religious issue was his motive, and one hundred years from now people would laugh at the actions taken by Waterbury's safety board. The newspapers quoted him as saying that he would rather be cursed today than laughed at tomorrow. He further noted that the World War had crushed an undemocratic nation only to use Prussian tactics at home.

On March 18, the local newspapers printed a small notice that the Civil Liberties Union had filed suit against Police Superintendent Beach in the amount of $10,000 for putting Carlo Tresca under "technical" arrest and preventing him from speaking. This, they contended, violated his right of free speech.

Two days later, the papers reported the resignation of Rabbi Browne from Temple Israel. He claimed that his resignation was already in the works but had been scheduled for June. The recent brouhaha aroused by Tresca's appearance in Waterbury only hastened that decision. That and the anger borne by several members of his most reputable and prominent congregation made a continued life in Waterbury uncomfortable for Browne.

Browne was well known as a local agitator and crusader. He complained about brothels and vice dens throughout the city. During his post-Waterbury years, he became known for compiling *The Graphic Bible* in 1928. This bible included map illustrations created by the then-unknown artist Mark Rothko, who was only twenty-five years old at the time. Browne proved himself untrustworthy when Macmillan published the book and Rothko's work was unrecognized. Browne's initials appear under the Rothko drawings. Rothko was enraged and filed suit.

Four artists testified that they had seen Rothko painting the drawings in the book, but Browne and Macmillan employed a stellar team of lawyers who created a hearing of great complexity and length. In the end, Rothko lost the case because a written contract wasn't in place. Though Browne won the suit, he lives on in history as an unsavory man who cheated a penniless genius.

Back in Waterbury, another date was set for Tresca to appear, and Rabbi Browne was in the midst of the notoriety.

On March 26, a small item appeared in the Waterbury papers. Tresca's third try at appearing in Waterbury was repulsed without his arrest when police officers formed a human wall at the door of the hall where Tresca was scheduled to appear. Tresca attempted to break through, but the officers held the line. Luigi Quintiliano of New York City, dubbed an "anti-fascist orator," was held for sedition after crying to the crowd that "freedom will never be attained until the red flag flies over the Statue of Liberty." He was held on $200,000 bond.

Over the course of six weeks, Carlo Tresca attempted to address the Italians in Waterbury three different times and was successfully repulsed. Those Italians opposing his appearance said that they had seen the hardship that strikes could bring to the average worker without many gains. With enough work to keep Waterbury workers busy, they didn't see the need to rile things up.

The Radium Girls

The *Waterbury Observer* ran a story by Ann Quigley in 2002 titled "After Glow." This article reported on the Waterbury Clock Company Radium Girls, whose health plights were revealed in the book *Deadly Glow* by Ross Mullner.

The tale of these girls began following World War I, when the Waterbury Clock Company introduced a wonderful glow-in-the-dark feature to watch faces. The radium paint applied to watch faces had served soldiers in the Great War, and now, in peacetime, the company found a tremendous civilian demand.

The Waterbury Clock Company was successful at cornering the market for affordable pocket watches. Its sales surged again when radium dials were introduced following World War I. *Postcard, author's collection.*

Young girls with nimble fingers and deft strokes hand-painted the numbers onto the watches, pointing their brushes perfectly with their lips between the strokes. It was a good, clean job prized by workers. And it was fun. Along with lips that glowed in the dark, the girls could bedeck their dresses and paint their finger- and toenails.

Millions of watches were produced during the heyday of the Roaring Twenties, so job security wasn't a problem. But there was a dark side that didn't surface until the girls grew sickly.

The *Observer* article introduced readers to seventeen-year-old Frances Splettstocher, who went to work in the Waterbury Clock Company on Cherry Street in 1921. Frances, like the other girls, had fun with the paint and never imagined that her life was at risk. Each day, she and the other girls bent over long workbenches, painting, putting brush to lips and growing used to the taste of the mix of glue and the naturally occurring radium in the paint.

She wasn't alone, nor were the girls of Waterbury. Other young women, just like them, were bent over workbenches in Orange, New Jersey, and Ottawa, Illinois, doing the same.

Ads like this ran nationally. The popularity of Waterbury watches increased with the inclusion of radium dials. *Author's collection.*

There had been rumblings about the radium, hints that it was not as safe as people imagined. But no one really listened. People wanted watches that glowed in the dark.

The best-known figure linked to radium was Madame Marie Curie, who, together with her husband Pierre, discovered the element. After Pierre had been killed in an accident in 1906, Marie Curie worked on the discovery alone, not patenting it so that the scientific community would have access to it and help with the process of utilizing it for humankind's benefit. That generosity of spirit was the hallmark of the Curies. After receiving the Nobel Prize, Pierre took his financial winnings and helped needy friends and students. In 1911, Marie won the Nobel Prize for Chemistry based on her discovery and work with radium.

The downside of radium began to show when Curie was hospitalized with depression and a kidney ailment. It wasn't until 1934 that this noteworthy scientist succumbed to aplastic anemia caused by radiation poisoning.

The link between the radioactivity of radium and health problems was not fully recognized at that time. In fact, radium was seen as healthful. Curie donated tubes of radon, gleaned from the radium in her storehouse, to ailing World War I soldiers in the field, providing doctors with the opportunity to take radiographies of bones (X-rays).

In a few short years, the uses for radium included glow-in-the-dark luminescence on watch faces. And the sickening of workers using the product became a way of studying side effects that would help in later years, when man began testing the atomic bomb.

In *Deadly Glow*, Mullner writes:

> *It was foolish to use radium, an element with a radioactive half-life of 1,600 years, on the dials of watches, which only lasted a year or two. Now, a new generation, which never used radium products, must face the health hazards and pay the enormous costs of cleaning up the wastes of the past.*

The paint used in Waterbury came from mixing glue with a yellow powder that contained radium and zinc sulfide. The radiation occurred through energy that made the zinc crystals flash with light—that's what caused the illumination. But now, people were beginning to learn the hidden properties of radium.

The girls at Waterbury Clock did piecework. This meant that their pay depended on how many dials they could complete. At eight cents per dial, a woman could earn as much as her dexterity, eyesight and craft would allow.

Some women completed thirty watch faces each day, while others were able to finish as many as three hundred.

With the necessity of pointing their brushes between dials, the best workers ingested the most amount of radium, putting them at a greater health risk.

Meanwhile, the medical community ignored potential risks and lauded radium as a modern marvel, a cure-all for arthritis, impotence and senility. Since it was naturally occurring, the supposition was that there was no harm in it. At the Radium Institute in New York, thousands of injections of the substance were distributed to wealthy patients who proclaimed the product a veritable fountain of youth.

While people were paying good money to be injected with the miracle element, Frances Splettstocher was plying her trade and getting radium for free. She still lived at home with her parents, three sisters and three brothers on Oak Street, and in 1925 she had been painting dials for four years. That was the year she began to feel weak and anemic. The left side of her face hurt, and her throat was sore. Soon, the pain moved into her teeth and jaw, forcing the young woman to see a dentist. When the doctor tried to alleviate the pain by pulling a tooth, a part of Frances's jaw came with it. Following that procedure, the tissue inside her mouth began to rot, eventually eating a hole through her cheek.

Her agony lasted a month before Frances succumbed. A funeral was held at St. Stanislaus Church, and her casket was laid to rest in Calvary Cemetery. The obituary that appeared in the *Waterbury Republican* read that the deceased "had a large circle of friends to whom the news of her death brings deep sorrow."

Frances entered Waterbury history by being the first of the Radium Girls to die. What caused her death was a mystery to her family and her physician.

In other states, Radium Girls were falling ill as Frances had. Severe toothaches and jaw problems caused teeth to be pulled and additional suffering as empty sockets failed to heal. Infection would set in and end up in necrosis, a condition where skin tissue dies.

In severe cases, jaws would rot away and have to be removed. Anemia and joint pain were more common.

In Orange, New Jersey, four women died in the same manner as Frances. Others, like Elizabeth Dunn of Waterbury, would experience spontaneous bone fractures in the extremities. The same year that claimed Frances, Elizabeth tripped on a dance floor. Despite never hitting the ground, her leg broke. Her death came two years later, in 1927, from jaw necrosis.

What actually happened to these women is better told in hindsight. Radium that was ingested entered the body. Since radium is chemically similar to calcium, it replaced calcium in the bones. Calcium is a strengthening agent, but radium provides a slow death to bone tissue. The reason why the mouth is the area to show the first symptoms is because it is the likeliest place for dead bone to become infected by bacteria. When the radium was ingested, alpha particles were introduced to the soft tissue within.

Radium emits three types of radiation—alpha, beta and gamma rays. Outside the body, alpha particles are the least dangerous. Though miniscule, they are bigger and bulkier than other forms of radiation, but once introduced into the body, their size keeps them in place and the energy they release affects the blood and organs.

In the 1920s, doctors were puzzled and diagnosed the women's ailments as trench mouth, ulcers and even syphilis. But the incidence of ailments centered on one profession begged another to look at the cause. New Jersey led the way in the investigation. The Orange plant had opened earlier than the one in Waterbury, so symptoms began showing up there long before Frances fell ill. In 1925, a group of dial painters sued U.S. Radium, a dial-painting studio. In September of that year, the *Journal of the American Medical Association* bolstered its contention when it linked the maladies claimed in the suit to radium poisoning.

The response to Frances's death, the New Jersey suit and the medical journal article was minimal from the Waterbury Clock Company. Rather than take a lucrative product off the market, the company hoped to keep its problems to a minimum by issuing an order for the girls to take a preventive approach and not to tip their brushes with their lips.

Frances's father also worked for the Waterbury Clock Company and was certain that his daughter's death was work-related, but he feared losing his job more than exposing the harm done to his daughter. After all, he had six other children to feed and clothe.

Two years later, Helen Wall joined Frances and Elizabeth Dunn, becoming the third girl to be killed by radium poisoning in Waterbury. This led to a period of upheaval for the company as it spent the next ten years paying almost $90,000 in compensation and medical costs for sixteen women. After that, $10,000 was put aside each year to cover additional costs.

Today, if a company took something that was, say, developed for use by astronauts and later was found to have helpful properties in civilian use and created a product that sold well because of its inclusion, would we think it dangerous? If NASA developed a lotion that soothed chafed skin caused by flight suits and it became a useful byproduct in makeup as a skin restorer, would we buy it? How about a food product or fabric? And if there were misgivings about a product, even warnings written on a label, would people eschew using it?

It is easy to say that this kind of tragedy can't happen today because product testing is far more rigorous. That is, in part, a result of the problems faced by people who lived and suffered in earlier years, when governments did not use so stringent a regulation system. Much of what we know today, especially about radiation poisoning, was gleaned from the experiences of the Radium Girls. What doctors learned about the properties of radium came from these victims, and this information was used to help others who, in the future, would work with radioactivity. Back then, even its inventor was puzzled. It was, after all, the cause of Marie Curie's own death.

The *Observer* article pointed out that the media failed in its responsibility to inform. Little was covered regarding the plight of these women. As a consequence, the courts did not receive cases, and boards of health were not notified about a public menace. In Waterbury, a company doctor handled the issue, and the company made quiet restitution. These women, as a result of the silence, went unheard.

Even with the scant knowledge of the time, changes were made—in favor of companies. The Workers Compensation Act made the eligible time frame for filing work-related cases three years instead of the previous five. Connecticut was pro-business and anti-labor. Women's leagues did not take up the cause either. Any compensation paid to the Connecticut women came with a nondisclosure clause. To get the money that they needed for medical help, the Waterbury girls had to keep quiet.

They faced the same brick wall other workers had come up against. Coal miners and asbestos workers faced similar hardships.

The typical cases for occupation-related diseases follows the pattern of workers getting sick, someone making a connection between the illness and the work and advocates working to get compensation and recognition. At each step, one can expect social resistance.

In New Jersey, the Consumers' League took up the cause of dial painters and helped bring the ailments of five workers to court. After a scientist prophesied that the girls would be dead within a year from radiation poisoning, the factory won an adjournment for fourteen months. Walter Lippmann, a notable journalist, was outraged by the callous disregard shown to the victims. He wrote in the *New York World*:

This is one of the most damnable travesties of justice that has ever come to our attention. It is an outrage that the company should attempt to keep these women from suing. It is an even greater outrage that Jersey justice should tease them along for 14 months before deciding whether they have the right to sue.

In 1928, that case was settled out of court. U.S. Radium did not accept liability but awarded each girl $10,000 and an annual pension of $600 to pay medical and legal expenses. The company claimed that the payoff was due to the inability to get a fair trial, not because it had done something wrong. The company's president's explanation for the entire fiasco was that dial workers were hired because they were physically unfit to handle other jobs. In short, no good deed went unpunished.

In total, thirty women died in Connecticut as a result of this process. Thirty-five succumbed in Illinois and forty-one in New Jersey. Some died young, like Frances, but others survived until much later, finally dying from bone or sinus cancer, leukemia or developed bone lesions. And some lived without a problem.

Cancer is not a disease that follows a traditional or projected route. If radiation comes into contact with thousands of cells, only one may be altered by the effect. And that change might be cancerous.

The process for dial painting was improved as a result of the early illnesses. Lip pointing was forbidden; hairnets, rubber gloves and fume hoods were adopted as safety precautions. Employees hired after improvements were implemented did not develop cancers directly related to the job. It was their early sisters who played the part of canaries in a coal mine.

The Waterbury Clock Company was one of only three major producers of the four million radium dial watches in the first year alone. The fad lasted ten years.

In 2002, the state inspected the site of the old factory to estimate what cleanup was necessary from radiation left behind. A total of $750,000 was allocated.

Today, the site includes apartments, businesses and abandoned buildings, and the health risk was nominal enough not to qualify for Superfund money distributed by the Environmental Protection Agency.

A partial list of victims who worked at the Waterbury Clock Company and their year of death was listed in the *Observer*. They would be unheard no more.

Frances Splettstocher, 1925
Elizabeth Dunn, 1927
Helen Wall, 1927
Mildred Williams Cardow, 1929
Marion Demolis, 1929
Louise Pine, 1931
Marjorie Domschott, 1931
Edith Lapiana, 1931 or '32
Mabel Adkins, 1934
Anna Mullenite, 1935
Florence Koss, 1935
Katherine Moore, 1936
Ethel Daniels, 1937

CHAPTER 4

POLITICS

Birth Control and the Catholic Church

The year 1938 was one of upset for Waterbury on two fronts. The most remembered is the T. Frank Hayes scandal, but the other involved the Chase Dispensary and birth control. Both incidents involved crimes of their day.

David J. Garrow devotes the entire first chapter of his book *Liberty & Sexuality* to how the roots of *Roe v. Wade* first took hold in Waterbury. This story links leading industrial families of progressive leanings, the family of the academy award–winning actress Katharine Hepburn, the American Medical Association, the Catholic Church and the leading local politicians and lawyers of their day. And it involved the poor working class in Waterbury who wanted some control over the size of their families.

To begin with, one must establish the role that the Catholic Church played in Waterbury. The city was the home of the founder of the Knights of Columbus and to-be-sainted Father McGivney. It had a population of over 70,000 immigrants and first- and second-generation Catholics. With an overall population of just shy of 100,000, this was a substantial Catholic enclave, and the priests in town wielded great power.

When the *Waterbury Democrat*, the town's more liberal paper, announced the opening of a birth control clinic, Catholic priests argued, in print, that they viewed birth control as a crime not dissimilar to illegal gambling.

The Chase Dispensary, which was named as the birth control clinic, emphasized dispensing information with regard to health issues; namely, if a woman were in mortal danger as a result of future pregnancies. The

The Catholic Church was a mainstay for myriad immigrants who settled in town to work. Birth control directly violated the church's teachings, and the clergy fought to have it banned in Waterbury. *Author's collection.*

Connecticut Birth Control League differed in that it believed that birth control information should be administered to any woman who requested it. The league felt that the Chase Dispensary was trying to adhere to the mores of the community leaders, hoping to stifle their censure.

That was not enough for the Catholic clergy, and they brought the matter to the Hartford Diocese, namely Bishop Maurice F. McAuliffe. Waterbury contained a fair amount of Catholic hierarchy within the town's borders. Monsignor Joseph Valdambrini served as pastor to Our Lady of Lourdes Church on South Main Street. His father was a Vatican banker with a royal title, according to Garrow. Father Eugene P. Cryne took the lead on this issue and made it clear that the church viewed birth control as immoral and that it was illegal by state law to dispense birth control information. Cryne dropped the hot potato into the lap of the state's attorney in Waterbury, William B. Fitzgerald, a practicing Catholic attached to St. Margaret's Parish.

Fitzgerald was following in the footsteps of his boss, Lawrence Lewis, who had been reprimanded for failing to prosecute illegal gambling practices within Waterbury social clubs. The Hayes trials were going on, and Fitzgerald had been pressured to step down, as had Lewis. Fitzgerald refused, and the need to prove that he was tough on crime, coupled with his Catholic upbringing, was favorable for the Catholic clergy in this instance.

The newspapers didn't let the matter fade away, and the clinic's administrators, Doctors B. Henry Mason and Charles L. Larkin, minimized the role that birth control issues played at the clinic. The newspaper reported that only 15 out of 250 women had received information of this nature. Judge Frank P. McEvoy, an active member of the Blessed Sacrament Parish, had a wife who had lobbied against any change in the laws that would allow birth control to be made legal. He granted a warrant to discover what was going on at the Chase Dispensary on Field Street, and the result was that law enforcement officials presented themselves at the closed clinic and confiscated materials. Following this raid, Dr. Mason would have to appear in court to explain why the seized diaphragms and other contraceptives should not be destroyed.

It is here in the story that things get dicey in a particularly parochial way. Fitzgerald was faced with a dilemma. The young Junior League volunteer who possessed the patient information cards was Virginia Goss, the wife of a prominent Scovill Brass executive. The cards contained private information, such as what patient received what form of contraceptive or advice. Fitzgerald also learned that the doctors he had been dealing with were not, in fact, the administrators of the Maternal Health Center (or birth control

The Chase Dispensary opened its doors to the birth control movement and was raided as a result. *Vicky Semrow.*

Catholicism was a predominant influence in Waterbury. The Immaculate Conception Church, now a basilica, dominates the town green. *Photo postcard, author's collection.*

clinic). The clinic was managed by his next-door neighbor and friend Clara Lee McTernan.

Goss's friend Dorothy Carmody revealed Fitzgerald's plan to acquire the patient cards. Carmody's husband was a prominent attorney in town and a friend of Fitzgerald's. Goss left town and secreted the information at her summer home on Fisher's Island, New York.

M. Heminway "Junie" Merriman Jr. was instructed by his boss, Ed Carmody, to get those cards back to Waterbury posthaste. Junie contacted Goss, who reluctantly handed them over to Ed Carmody's firm, which ultimately handed them over to Fitzgerald. The task then became finding a good lawyer to represent the Connecticut Birth Control League (CBCL) in Waterbury.

That task fell to Warren Upson, a prominent attorney who represented William J. Pape and the *Republican-American* newspaper in the T. Frank Hayes corruption investigation.

Prior to this local incident, Fitzgerald knew that he was wrangling with not only the Catholic Church, but also serious female crusaders who believed in disseminating birth control. Margaret Sanger spent a month in prison for her convictions. This was a case that was shaping up into a battle, and he would be facing people whom he would have to look in the eye every day that he remained in Waterbury.

The crux of the birth control law stemmed from the year 1879 and was supposed to aid in the suppression of vice. Bridgeport representative to the Connecticut Assembly P.T. Barnum (not exactly remembered as a bastian of moral rectitude) headed a committee that fine-tuned the ban on birth control. The bill made it illegal to traffic in or use any materials or drugs deemed obscene or that would prevent conception.

The debate gained momentum in the 1920s, and it was here in Waterbury, in the year 1938, that the test case went to court. The women who advocated a woman's right to decide how many children she would bear saw the opposition as hypocrites. Waterbury had its fair share of large families, a trend that continued into the 1960s, but there were many families that had too few children for the parents not to have been "breaking the law."

Waterbury's clinic was not the first of its kind, nor was it the first to go to court. But its purpose hit the public's awareness at a time when the local press was keen to report. The Hayes scandal had whetted the appetite of the writers, and with all eyes on Waterbury's political scene, it made sense to make hay out of another quarter.

The formal medical community (the AMA) sat on the fence. While it could not condemn birth control for medical reasons, it did not embrace the woman's choice movement that was gaining momentum throughout the country. In 1937, supporters of birth control within the ranks succeeded in changing that policy to one in which it would be ethical to disseminate the best methods of birth control. Connecticut opened four clinics that would provide that service. The Chase Dispensary in Waterbury was one key location.

In January 1938, Anne Chase Hart, a member of one of Waterbury's leading families, approached leaders of the Waterbury medical community. They reacted favorably, and prominent women of Waterbury were asked to support this endeavor. Edith Chase, Mildred Chase Ely, Florence Chase, Ruth Northrup and twenty-eight others attended a meeting about whether a birth control clinic should be installed in town. The participants agreed that it would be a political matter, and one that would evoke the displeasure of the Catholic clergy, but a month's reflection on the matter and a second meeting would give them time to carefully weigh the consequences and mull over the benefits.

The legal issues were the overriding reason that the women hesitated to fund a clinic—that and the cost. The second meeting was only twenty-two strong, but among those attending were medical personnel, ministers, a social worker and a personnel officer from Scovill Brass. Leah Cadbury from the Connecticut Birth Control League was encouraged by the quality of the turnout, especially since the weather was bad. But the negatives were outweighing the positives, until Clara Lee McTernan suggested that Waterbury provide transportation for local women to go to Hartford to get birth control information directly from the Hartford clinic. Millicent Pond from Scovill Brass volunteered to do the driving.

Clara Lee McTernan was the wife of Charles McTernan, who founded the McTernan School for Boys. Clara had been a nurse in New Jersey and spent a summer working at a summer camp run by McTernan and his first wife. After the first Mrs. McTernan died, Charles married Clara Lee and moved her to Waterbury, where she worked at his Columbia Boulevard school. McTernan was sixteen years her senior and had two grown sons in college.

Armed with a list of one hundred names of potential clients from Waterbury, McTernan contacted ministers and directors of welfare agencies to garner the three-dollar fee per patient that the clinic in Hartford would charge. During the first month of operation, she hoped to transport four people.

The Chase women did not want to become as personally active as had McTernan, but they were persuaded to make some financial contributions. It was decided that because the Chase Dispensary already had a Maternal Health Service, it might not be necessary to open an independent one—that would eliminate the onerous task of fundraising. The obstacle was approaching the hospital board to allow the Connecticut Birth Control League access to the Chase Dispensary to disseminate birth control materials without actually stating that was their purpose.

Massachusetts, meanwhile, was active in pursuing legal remedies to halt the spread of birth control and its clinics. In October 1938, the U.S. Supreme Court overruled the appeal of the Massachusetts Birth Control League, letting stand the convictions of the defendants taken in a raid on the Salem clinic.

A small number of women, meanwhile, were receiving medical advice and contraceptives in Waterbury, using the transport system initiated by McTernan.

Newspapers latched onto the Waterbury story but had difficulty getting people to speak on the record. Fitzgerald was playing his hand close to the vest, and hospital officials were wondering how to gracefully back away from the whole mess. At best, they wanted to be nothing more than landlords.

Fitzgerald was planning to prosecute, but he didn't know exactly who would be the defendant. Potential targets included the CBCL officials and clinic personnel. Fitzgerald told his former boss, who had come in to the office to discuss the matter, that he could overlook the information being disseminated because of health motives, but that it did not appear that any of the patients had health concerns dire enough to warrant that advice. What Fitzgerald was trying to figure out was who actually owned the contraceptive devices—the league, the clinic or individuals?

Upson received word from his legal circles that the recent Supreme Court case upholding the Salem clinic decision would work against him in Connecticut. His job kept getting harder as Sallie Pease, president of the league in Hartford, publicly stated that she welcomed the case in order to open the discussion and overturn the antiquated Connecticut law of 1879.

A meeting took place in Newtown that brought the potential defendants together. Margaret Sanger, Kit Hepburn and other league officers; Clara McTernan; and legal advisors for all met to plot out the strategy with Upson.

When the first hearing was held, a bag and two boxes filled with contraceptive materials were hauled before the judge, who examined some of the objects within. The hospital had disavowed ownership, and Upson was ordered to reveal the local league officers affiliated with the clinic. Goss, McTernan and Harriet Griggs were offered. It was then that Clara McTernan was deposed by her neighbor, Bill Fitzgerald.

Her testimony helped to put some distance between the league and the hospital administration. Women could not simply walk into the clinic, McTernan said. They had to be referred by a doctor, and that was a matter between doctor and patient.

Fitzgerald then demanded to know who financed the operation since it was clear by the clinic's records that the women attending the clinic were not supporting it. The finances showed a total of ninety-six dollars worth of income, with only ten dollars being supplied by patients. McTernan affirmed this and listed that Edith Chase, Lucy Burrall, Mary Burrall, Edward and Edith Davis and Deborah Elton had financially contributed.

Fitzgerald asked McTernan if she believed that she had done something illegal. The former nurse answered that, no, she did not think it was illegal for a doctor to give advice to a patient.

This hearing left Upson with little doubt that his clients would face criminal charges, and the league created a five-member executive council to determine how the CBCL would proceed. The members were Sallie Pease and Kit Hepburn of the state organization; Upson as Waterbury legal advisor; gynecologist A. Nowell Creadick; and Bridgeport attorney Johnson Stoddard.

Former nurse Clara McTernan and Doctors Bill Goodrich and Roger Nelson went before Judge Kenneth Wynne, where they were formally arrested and pleaded not guilty.

Kenneth Wynne was politically savvy, having been the executive secretary to Governors Simeon Baldwin in 1914–15 and Wilbur Cross in 1931–35. He was particularly sensitive to the political overtones, as well as the undercurrents, and refused Fitzgerald's demand that each be held on $500 bond. Wynne released all three to Upson.

At the crux of this case was whether the 1879 law only covered, as Fitzgerald and the Catholics claimed, obscene literature and not health issues.

Fitzgerald had honed in on patients at the clinic who were young mothers who had, on average, one birth a year. He contended that the contraceptives they received were not to prevent a medical hardship but a matter of convenience. He remained silent about the case during the preparation, leaving the defense team wondering what he was going to cite. Fitzgerald further kept Upson off kilter by refusing to return the patients' cards. This meant that the CBCL had to visit with each clinic patient in order to reconstruct vital data.

Upson filed a fifty-four-page brief that clarified the 1879 law as dealing only with obscene literature and agreeing that the immoral and unlawful use of contraceptives that were not medically prescribed was wrong. He also agreed that disseminating birth control literature to high school–age girls was also wrong in that it broke down the barrier that the fear of pregnancy conveyed. Freedom, he argued, was the key point. Why should government restrict people's conduct if that conduct only involved a person's own body and did not infringe on the rights of others? He argued that people had the right to begin or deter pregnancy, but that this right was in opposition to abortion. Fitzgerald countered with his own brief, citing other states' practices and laws.

The CBCL was overjoyed when Wynne rejected Fitzgerald's brief because it erred in comparing Connecticut to Massachusetts. In Massachusetts, where the Salem clinic was raided, it was illegal to distribute contraceptive devices. In Connecticut, the law prohibited their use.

Kit Hepburn was quoted in the press as calling Wynne "wise and humane," but not everybody saw him that way. The following Sunday, the Catholic pulpits rang with condemnation of Wynne's verdict.

Upson did not encourage Clara McTernan to reopen the clinic but urged her, instead, to raise funds for the Hartford clinic, where Waterbury women could still go for help. It was essential, he believed, that the poor were not punished for Waterbury's parochial leanings.

He then made a bold move to have the case thrown out by going to a judge who would soon be leaving Waterbury through a natural rotation. He approached Judge John A. Cornell to solve the problem before leaving the area.

Cornell surprised Upson with his opinion. He didn't agree with Judge Wynne and did not believe that the three defendants were acting in a professional capacity when distributing contraceptives. Now that the matter was in his hands, he sat on the case for six long weeks, much to the consternation of both sides.

Frustrated, Upson and Fitzgerald joined forces and went to Hartford to complain to Chief Justice of Connecticut William M. Maltbee. Maltbee was, by reputation, a fair and easygoing man, and he gently nudged Cornell without luck.

Upson appealed to Fitzgerald to drop the charges so as not to jeopardize the doctors' medical licenses and their ability to earn a living. Fitzgerald could not comply without angering the church.

Maltbee tired of Cornell's procrastination and assigned Wynne to make judgments for the three defendants. On November 11, 1938, he found all not guilty within five minutes' time.

Upson felt some ease that his clients would not be going to jail, but Fitzgerald was threatening to appeal. The following January, Fitzgerald argued that appeal before the Connecticut Supreme Court of Errors, and when Upson looked upon the five-man panel, his heart sank. All were older men, with the two youngest being fifty-seven years of age. All were Protestant and Republican. Their conservatism was legendary. Four had been legislators, and one had assisted in the legislature. All served on the superior court.

Outside the court, the other Connecticut clinics remained open and operational. The press wrote favorable stories about the benefits of the clinics and their moral strictures.

On March 20, the decision was handed down. In the case of *The State of Connecticut v. Roger B. Nelson et al.*, there was a three-to-two ruling to uphold the 1879 statute as construed by the prosecutor. The three defendants could be prosecuted. This was how Waterbury stood in the center of the great Connecticut birth control debate.

By 1947, things hadn't changed much according to a report in *Time* magazine. A sixty-eight-year-old blue law in Connecticut continued to make it a misdemeanor for a doctor to advise, or a citizen to practice, birth control. Though it was seldom enforced, doctors had tried eleven different times to repeal it. This year, it was tried again.

Doctors formed a "Committee of 100" to sponsor a bill permitting a doctor to give birth control information to a patient. It would not matter whether the woman's health was at risk. This time, they were armed with support from the *Hartford Courant* newspaper, five hundred ministers and an Elmo Roper poll that showed that 85 percent of the state's citizens supported the bill in principle. Of the citizens taking the poll, 75 percent were Roman Catholic.

A battle raged in the press leading up to the vote. Roman Catholic hospitals in Waterbury, Bridgeport and Stamford upped the ante by firing six members of the Committee of 100. Father Lawrence Skelly explained, "The [hospital's] action was self-defensive…You gave your name publicly to the support of a movement which is directly opposed to the code under which the hospital operates."

As a result of this action, the Hartford Ministers' Association and the Plainville Council of Churches passed resolutions urging the state to withhold aid and tax exemptions from the Roman Catholic hospitals.

Doctors viewed this as a threat against free speech on medical subjects.

Despite the city's best efforts to curb the practice, birth control has become mainstream, with some contraception being sold in supermarkets, over the counter. And in the *Roe v. Wade* decision, abortion, too, became legal. In Waterbury, however, the protests against the practice were regular and faithful.

The Great Toilet Scandal

Looking back from the twenty-first century, we see that political corruption is not new to Waterbury. From the 1980s on, two mayors have gone to jail, one mayor was indicted and then acquitted and a former governor was imprisoned. But before then, T. Frank Hayes was the poster child for corruption.

It was a humid day on August 16, 1939, when the jury retired from the courtroom to deliberate the fate of twenty-seven defendants. Judge Ernest Inglis was presiding in the Kendrick Avenue courthouse. Rosalind Russell, the famous movie actress, was in the audience, home for vacation and sitting with her brother James. The public spilled over to the outside as this nine-month-long case came to an end.

It took six hours and thirty-two minutes for the jury to declare the verdict of guilty for all.

What ended in 1939 began much earlier, even before Hayes took office. The previous mayor, Francis P. Guilfoile, who served from 1922 to 1930, set the stage. In 1921, Guilfoile claimed that the city was in debt and had a deficit of $1.5 million, floating bonds to start fresh. Eight years later, when he left office, the debt rose to $16 million, with a deficit of $4 million. The Great Depression had begun, and Waterbury was in dire financial straits.

T. Frank Hayes won the election over Guilfoile by promising fiscal reform. He was a dashing figure, splendid in his white hats and later known for riding a white steed in local parades. He was a popular, ruddy man of quick wit.

His first order of business was to bond the $4 million deficit. An audit of the previous administration revealed that Guilfoile had irregularities with contracts, excessive payments to contractors and illegal payments to city officers. The state legislature investigated and found the bookkeeping to be sloppy, and though it hinted at criminality, no charges were brought. But Hartford was eager to see Waterbury back on track. The state recognized the burden the country's economic downturn would place on its cities.

Hayes assumed office with the hope that he could live up to his promises of reform, and the state granted him leeway to alleviate the burden he had inherited. One of his first priorities was to revamp the city charter with a "strong mayor" provision. This gave the mayor full responsibility for city transactions, overseeing the ethics of city employees and hiring and firing at will.

With a 41.90 mill rate, the public hoped that Hayes would prove to be a good, strong mayor who would put the city back on track. The change was made in the charter, and Hayes began to work.

Hayes proved to be a quick study and implemented changes almost immediately. Some of those changes were hidden from the public's scrutiny. In one case, in which Hayes saved the city money, the savings came at the expense of education. Approximately 1.5 percent of the mill rate was set by the legislature in Hartford and earmarked for building schools. Hayes siphoned off the school money into the general budget.

This courthouse holds a lot of history within its walls. Courts in Waterbury saw a fair share of trials and political shenanigans. *Photo postcard, author's collection.*

The first year, Hayes had to fork over $100,000 for bond payments. He sent the legislature half the amount, banking on its goodwill to fund the rest. He was right, and Connecticut's taxpayers assumed the burden.

In 1935, Hayes was elected lieutenant governor while still serving as Waterbury's mayor under Governor Wilbur Cross. Two years later, the legislature allowed Waterbury to float $2 million in bonds for the infrastructure. The money was allocated by the Works Progress Administration (WPA) and earmarked for work relief, increasing the city's bonded debt to $18 million.

Another example of Hayes's manipulation involved the Mutual Aid Society established in Waterbury to help the poor hit by the Depression. Workers were asked to pledge 1 to 3 percent of their pay, with employers matching that contribution. Many people willingly complied.

Hayes saw the response from people and implemented a plan for city employees in which they would return between 5 and 20 percent of their pay.

Hayes was, if anything, a quick and nimble study in the methods of acquiring more money for his budget. Once the dollars were in hand, they were doled out to Hayes's supporters.

With broad changes that appeared as reform, Hayes's popularity with the voters grew. When he took office, he garnered a seven-hundred-vote lead. By 1937, his nine-thousand-vote lead in the previous election had dropped to seventeen hundred, and Sherwood Rowland defeated his comptroller, Daniel Leary.

The *Republican-American* newspaper led the investigation into Hayes in 1933, after hearing stories of employee misuse and the distribution of goods to individuals favorable to Hayes.

Real evidence was made manifest when Sherwood Rowland took office in 1938. Gaining the position with only a thirty-three-vote lead, he set to work and uncovered a mare's-nest of problems. He took those problems to state attorney Lawrence Lewis and asked for a grand jury and an out-of-town prosecutor to investigate the corruption that was running rampant in city government. Rowland's evidence was enough to convince the state, and it put Hugh Mead Alcorn Jr., Harold Mitchell and County Detective Edward Hickey in charge.

Stories began to surface of reprisals against enemies of Hayes and complaints against the city. City employees feared for their jobs. Taxpayers were at the mercy of the city assessors—any trouble and the mayor had your property reassessed at a greater value. Complaints cost money and people kept silent.

The initial findings were enough to empanel an extraordinary grand jury, which issued a seventy-five-page report and twenty-seven arrest warrants. The defendants included:

T. Frank Hayes, mayor and lieutenant governor
Daniel Leary, comptroller
Thomas Kelly, executive secretary
Simon Alderman
Martin Dunn, an employee in the comptroller's office
Charles O'Connor, from the City's Corporation Counsel
Thomas Fleming, superintendent of streets
Timothy Horgan, city hall superintendent
Thomas Shanahan, city assessor
John Crary, city assessor
Michael Slavin, deputy registrar of voters
Henry Minor, chair police commission
Carl Olsen, banker
Charles Williamson, lobbyist
Harry MacKenzie, lobbyist
George Kingsley, New York auditor
Enoch Borgnaes, Kingsley's employee
William Murray, Kingsley's partner
John Meany, Kingsley's partner
John Johnston, New York broker
John Purdie, New York City private detective
Frank Santalucia, Waterbury contractor
Phil Coppeto, Waterbury contractor
James Healey, contractor
Edward Levy, New Haven attorney
Ralph Coppeto, attorney
Donato Pietrarona (Dan Peters), Bristol innkeeper

The men initially arrested were whittled down to twenty-two. The courts freed Ralph Coppeto. William Murray, Michael Slavin and Timothy Horgan pleaded nolo contendere. Enoch Borgnaes became a fugitive.

Harry MacKenzie, Edward Levy and Charles Williamson agreed to testify for the state.

What was revealed was sickening to the Waterbury voters, who had placed their trust in Hayes. When the Waterbury paper launched an exposé about the Hayes administration prior to the election, soon-to-be-ousted Daniel Leary approached the paper's attorney, Warren Upson, with a deal. Leary promised that if the newspaper eased up on its campaign against him, he wouldn't reveal the findings of a New York detective that were detrimental to both Upson and the paper. The deal was refused and the stories were printed, leading to the election upset.

Voter fraud was one subject dear to the newspaper's heart. It exposed how registered loyal Democrats were also being listed as Republicans to offset the numbers. Upson and publisher William Pape challenged the city's practice in court and won.

The seventy-five-page report issued by the grand jury estimated that the amount of money illegally spent in Waterbury was in the millions. The "rampant corruption" it cited included bribes, payments and kickbacks for imaginary projects and services—self-serving investments. Lore in town today includes the $100,000 landscaping for the newly built municipal stadium. The cost rose to that amount because of the supposed need for continually replacing stolen trees and shrubs.

Most corruption cases that involve money can be overwhelming to the public. Trying to discover who spent what, where, why and how seemed to be a rehash of the Guilfoile years. In order to capture the media's and the public's attention, a political corruption story needs a hook, and the Hayes trial had one—toilets.

It is not every day that a toilet can be the center of controversy, but in the Hayes trial that is exactly what it did become.

The scandal began with the Merritt Parkway, a scenic route leading westward through southern Connecticut to New York. Hayes was serving as lieutenant governor when he learned of a public toilet that would clean itself. The item had a self-retracting seat that was cleaned with live steam and a scrubbing brush between uses, then cooled for the next user. Hayes believed that it was an idea worth investing in, and he promptly did so. He then insured his bet by presiding over the legislation that would have made the product mandatory in all public buildings along the Merritt Parkway. It came under the guise of a health bill, and several other legislators were involved.

The corruption case would have been bad enough on a local level, but the fact that Hayes's shenanigans transcended to Hartford made him even more memorable.

Two for One

Hayes's trial didn't put an end to political shenanigans. In July 1949, *Time* magazine reported a Waterbury incident that should have passed unnoticed. Six habitual drinkers were brought before the bench. But this time, things were different.

Two complete sets of judges were on the job. Republican judges appointed by the outgoing Republican regime were still working, though temporarily. Democratic Governor Chester Bowles had appointed a new set of Democrats to replace the outgoing judges. What was different is that, this time, a 131-year-old law was employed to adjourn the legislature. Once the legislators were gone, the governor made his 129 judicial appointments, creating an awkward overlap.

Bowles made the bold move to aggravate the uncooperative Republican House of Representatives, which opposed his New Deal ways.

Cities handled the overload differently. Norwalk divvied up the cases, with Democrats handling odd number cases and Republicans, even. New London Democrats set up their own court and dismissed all cases on the docket before Republican Judge Louis C. Wool could convene.

A temporary compromise had to be implemented across the state, leaving the final decision of who would stay and who would go to the state Supreme Court.

As for the Waterbury drunkards, they explained their inebriation this way: "We were celebrating the appointment of the Democratic judges." Republican Judge Charles Summa gave them ten days.

CHAPTER 5

PEOPLE JUST GET MAD

A Neighborly Dispute

Many like to reminisce about the 1950s as a time of goodwill in which we lived harmoniously with our neighbors—a more genteel way of life. That wasn't always the case.

Time magazine reported, in July 1950, an incident in which two Waterbury neighbors on Long Hill resolved their dispute.

Alice Fox and Katherine Rollo lived next door to each other in a housing development. Whatever started the argument wasn't clear, but the magazine reported that it ended when Fox kicked Rollo in the stomach with enough force to land the fallen woman in the hospital for six days.

Alice was arrested and fined twenty-five dollars for breach of peace, but rather than feeling ashamed of her notoriety, she felt vindicated. Alice Fox was thirty-two years old at the time.

Katherine did not feel that the matter was over and sued her former friend in civil court. She won a $1,200 judgment, and Alice agreed to pay $2 a week.

The plaintiff did not agree to let the matter linger that long, and so Katherine dug into a colonial Connecticut law to settle things more quickly. Under the Body Execution Law, Alice was remitted to the New Haven County jail, sentenced to serve one day for every dollar unpaid to Katherine Rollo. In addition, Alice was forced to pay ten dollars to the county for room and board. It was a modern version of debtors' prison.

Rollo didn't let up. While Alice was languishing away in the hoosegow, the satisfied Katherine Rollo watched Fox's husband struggle to care for three youngsters. She was so happy at the sight that she would spontaneously break into song—"The Prisoner's Song," to be exact.

Alice Fox served only forty-seven days in jail, however. She, too, took advantage of an antiquated Connecticut law called the Poor Debtor's Oath. She swore to possessing less than seventeen dollars in assets, thus enabling her to avoid the unpaid judgment.

Fox finally returned home, and *Time* did not report whether either family moved or constructed a "good neighbor" fence.

The Mad Bomber

Terror is not new to New York City, and the Unabomber Ted Kaczynski wasn't the first to attack innocent people with bombs.

George Metesky lived in the Brooklyn section of Waterbury, and he used his sister's home to hide in plain sight while he wrought sixteen years of fear and uncertainty in New York.

For a period of time beginning in 1940 and lasting until 1956 (with a sabbatical from terror during World War II), the quiet man left bombs in public places—phone booths, train stations, movie theatres. The first incident took place in the offices of Con Ed, New York City's public utility. A toolbox was left in an office. Inside the box was a pipe bomb, along with a note that read, "Con Edison crooks, this is for you." No fingerprints were ever found.

Metesky had worked for the precursor to Con Ed, United Electric and Power, and was terminated following an accident at work. Following this, Metesky contracted tuberculosis, leaving the unemployed man angry.

When war broke out and no new bombs were delivered, the case lost momentum and fizzled. A year later, however, another pipe bomb was discovered at a Con Ed location. This time, the bomb was hidden inside an old sock and contained no note.

Metesky wrote to the police three months later, stating, "I will make no more bomb units for the duration of the War—My patriotic feelings have made me decide this—Later I will bring the Con Edison to justice—they must pay for the dastardly deeds."

This was the first of many letters sent over the course of nine years. They were sent to the Con Ed office, individuals, the police, newspapers and movie houses. All were signed with the initials "F.P." (Metesky revealed later that "F.P." stood for "Fair Play.")

When the war ended, the real terror at home began when bombs were discovered throughout the city. During the years between 1950 and 1956, more than thirty bombs were left in phone booths, libraries, subway stations and cinemas.

Metesky, or the "Mad Bomber" as he was known in the press, placed the bombs himself. In the case of movie houses, he would buy a ticket and then place the bomb on an empty seat while the lights were down. He would also slit the fabric of the seat cover and slip the bomb inside before heading out an emergency door.

It wasn't until December 2, 1956, that police began a massive manhunt that would end in Metesky's arrest. That was the night Metesky planted a bomb in the Paramount Theatre in Brooklyn, New York. Approximately fifteen hundred people filled the seats when an explosion ripped through the theatre, injuring six patrons, three of them seriously.

The police realized that the Mad Bomber's devices were growing more sophisticated. The bombs were also being placed in more densely populated areas. Things were escalating.

Without a war to cover, newspapers began reporting on the failure to apprehend the public menace. Citizens became outraged and fearful.

Leads were few. Without fingerprints or a reliable postmark, the New York Police Department tried something new—profiling.

Dr. James Brussel was a psychiatrist for Manhattan who had begun working with the theory that criminals had behavioral patterns. He was called in on the case and addressed a group of doubtful officers. The doctor informed them that the criminal would be a middle-aged white man who was Catholic and of Slavic descent. The Mad Bomber would be a meticulous sort who was self educated. An Oedipal complex was tossed into the mix, meaning that the culprit would be living with a female relative. Also, the doctor claimed, he lived in Connecticut.

Brussel advised that the Mad Bomber had initially targeted Con Ed and so must have been a former employee. Searches through personnel records would be fruitful. He recommended publicizing the profile.

Before the detectives left, Dr. Brussel added one more thing—the Mad Bomber would be wearing a buttoned-up, double-breasted suit when captured.

Profiling at that time was not the science that is depicted on television today. The New York detectives of 1956 must have thought the good doctor was simply speculating, banking on the odds of being right. But they also recognized that they were desperate for leads.

It wasn't long before the Mad Bomber responded to the news coverage about the profile. In an arrogant letter to the *Journal-American*, Metesky documented his accident and the ensuing compensation case. Con Ed employee Alice Kelly matched the employee file with the case Metesky outlined. Detectives now had a serious lead to follow, straight to Connecticut.

Metesky was apprehended in Waterbury in the Brooklyn neighborhood home that he shared with his two unmarried sisters, Anna and Mae. When the law descended in force, it was early morning, and George was not wearing a double-breasted suit but a bathrobe, appropriate for the early hour.

The police took a tour of the garage workshop, where they found bomb parts, while Metesky went to his room to change. He emerged in a double-breasted suit.

The former utility employee explained that the injury he suffered at work cost him thousands of dollars, and he had not received any compensation. The injury occurred in 1931 at the Hellgate plant, where Metesky stated that he had inhaled gas fumes that left him disabled. United Electric and Power rejected his compensation claim, not because it was deemed false, but because it had not been filed in a timely manner. The original employer merged with Con Ed some years later. His initial target was Con Ed, not the innocent people who found themselves near the bombs.

The New York court system judged that George Metesky was paranoid, and he was committed to an insane asylum until 1974. Dr. Brussel visited the infamous Mad Bomber at times. It had been his first major profile, and it led to the doctor's participation in such notorious cases as that of the Boston Strangler.

Upon his release in 1974, Metesky returned to Waterbury and spent his remaining years living quietly, a fixture at the Silas Bronson Library, where he sat and read throughout the day. He died in 1994 at the age of ninety. He still holds the record for the number of bombs left throughout New York City.

The ancillary interest in the case was how a psychiatrist could have so accurately profiled the bomber without having seen him. What was in the letters that led to so detailed a description?

Brussel's deductions came from whittling down the facts and narrowing down the prospects. Women rarely make bombs, and so that cut the number of suspects approximately in half. Paranoid individuals are more prone to this type of behavior. Paranoiacs hold grudges and feel persecuted. They resent criticism and often feel superior to others. Since most paranoia comes to full bloom by age forty, Brussel surmised that the first bomb would have been planted at that age and, therefore, the bomber would be in his mid-fifties.

Paranoids are loners, and so it was unlikely that the bomber would be married. Subtle clues within the letters indicated a sexual inadequacy to the doctor. That clue was Metesky's handwriting. It contained squared capitals, with the exception of *w*'s, whose bottom two bumps were rounded like a woman's breasts.

Brussel also predicted that Metesky would be muscular. He relied on one German study, which stated that 85 percent of paranoids were athletic and stocky.

The vocabulary and grammar within the letters led to the idea that the bomber would be educated. As for ethnicity, Eastern Europeans had a greater population of bombers than other regions. If, indeed, he was an Eastern European or Slav, he would be Roman Catholic. Slavs were family oriented, so if unmarried, it was more likely for Metesky to live with a female relative—a mother, sister or aunt.

Though the bomber's letters were postmarked from Westchester County, Brussel concluded that an intelligent man would travel away from his true origin in order to throw off the police. In this case, Metesky would mail the letters en route by train from Connecticut to Manhattan.

Pain and suffering were repeated throughout the bomber's missals, and Brussel predicted that the author had experience with illness or injury. He had, mistakenly, assumed that it would be a heart ailment, as the age and ethnicity would suggest.

As for the double-breasted suit, Brussel determined that the paranoid bomber, being a fastidious individual, would wear a proper form of suit.

CHAPTER 6

THE UNDERBELLY

Sin City

In any city where people have jobs and money to spend, you'll find gambling, prostitution and other vices hidden away. Sometimes they weren't so hidden. One city attorney recalls his childhood in the 1950s, when, across from the Century Gate on East Main Street, three different bookies did business in the backrooms of what seemed like legitimate shops.

Donnelly remembers one day when Charlie Summa raced out the back door of his shop, across the yard and tried to hoist himself up a concrete wall to escape the police raid within.

It was during the 1950s that *STAG* magazine did a story on what it dubbed "Sin City" (Waterbury), where the local farm boys from the surrounding suburbs could roll into town with money to burn and spend it on strip clubs, hookers and private gambling dens. In 1954, *STAG* reported that Waterbury was a "triple-plated, grade-A sin pit."

It was a slur that, in some circles, was well deserved. From the earliest days of bright lights and burlesque, Waterbury held allure as a place where desires could be satisfied. Of course, today, no one has any personal memories to share, but the legends are fun.

The most common and colorful is about a horse. There are two versions. The first has a horse stabled at what became the public comfort station that is now situated behind Drescher's Restaurant. The horse, it is told, was trained to take gentlemen, no matter how inebriated, to the local brothel on Pearl Lake Road.

Waterbury's history as a "Sin City" included myriad bars, even during Prohibition. This photo was taken at Sheehy's Grill on Hamilton Avenue. *Author's collection.*

Entertainment centered on East Main Street. At night, the street was aflame with marquees. *Photo postcard, author's collection.*

Downtown was a bustling city. With this growth, however, came corruption. *Photo postcard ca. 1930s, author's collection.*

The second version has the horse belonging to a family man whose secret vice was revealed when the horse inadvertently turned toward the brothel while transporting the family to church.

Who knows if either is true, but both versions are entertaining.

One true tale that began in 1961 involved a Waterbury con artist with a keen mind and an engaging wit. Tommy Speers began his career with a stint as an employee at the local newspaper. His job was to receive and collate the sports scores. It wasn't long before Speers used his position to edit the scores in his favor.

He later graduated to police informer during the 1970s, using his association with the state police as a cover for his gambling habits. As the first informant of the organized crime squad, he would hang out at a bar suspected of illegal gambling and place a few small bets, gradually working his way into the bookie's favor for larger lines of credit. When he lost big, he didn't have to worry about paying up—he'd simply turn the operation over to the police.

Waterbury became too hot for Speers, and he moved on to surrounding towns. The *Hartford Courant* ran a story at the time of his death in 2001 that recounted one scam in which Speers approached a liquor store owner with a proposition. He told the businessman that he had been a liquor shop owner on the Cape and had set fire to the place for the insurance money. He offered the inventory at a good price but asked for money upfront to cover expenses. When the time came to deliver, Speers arrived with a newspaper story outlining a police impoundment of bootleg liquor. No liquor, according to the report, ever existed. Speers used his newspaper experience to phone in the bogus story to a small, local paper. He posed as a state trooper to verify the story.

The charm of Speers was always short-lived. His association with the Connecticut State Police ended bitterly in 1973, when they were asked to stake out a meeting Speers arranged with a gambler and his enforcers. An argument led to shooting, and one of the enforcers was killed.

Justice finally caught up with Tommy Speers in the late 1980s, when he was arrested in Waterbury for gambling. He was sentenced to a short stint in prison.

Waterbury was a mecca for fun, drawing people to its many burlesque theatres and nightclubs. *Photo postcard, author's collection.*

Racial Strife

The history of Connecticut doesn't emphasize slavery, and many residents with a rudimentary interest in history associate the institution with the pre–Civil War agrarian South. But New England was generally the last market for slaves captured in Africa. Once the heartiest and youngest men and women were sold off to work the cane fields of the islands and the cotton fields of the South, the weaker slaves were carted north and sold on the auction block in towns like Middletown.

Deacon Stephen Bronson of Waterbury owned "Dick the Slave," who would regale the Bronson family children with stories of his capture as a boy in Africa. He spent his entire adult life working in Waterbury until his death in 1835 at age ninety.

Henry Bronson's 1858 *History of Waterbury* was the earliest account of slaves in Waterbury. He explained that the low number of slaves held in town was a matter of practicality. The earliest settlers were very poor, and if a family managed to scrape together the price of a slave, they were saddled with the burden of keeping that slave in food, clothing and shelter. The amount of help a slave could provide in a climate with long winters was nominal compared to Southern climes. The winter months had to be spent in a productive manner, and that meant training a slave to do indoor chores.

Mingo was the first to come to Waterbury in 1730, and he was owned by Deacon Thomas Clark. Bronson wrote:

> *His master used to let him out for hire by the day, first to drive plow, then to work with the team. At Clark's death in 1764, Mingo was allowed to choose which of the sons he would live with. He preferred to remain at the old homestead with Thomas; but after the latter commenced keeping tavern, he did not like his occupation and went to reside with Timothy on Town Plot. He had a family and considerable property and died in 1800.*

When the Revolution began, slaves volunteered for the Continental army but were rejected. When British troops promised freedom to any slave joining the English, the colonists reconsidered. As a result, General George Washington had under his command nearly five thousand black soldiers. Mingo was one.

Slaves had another difference, aside from being black. Unlike their white neighbors, slaves were called by a single name—like Mingo. Captain William

Hickox had two slaves called Fortune and Dinah; Parson Southmayd owned Samson and Phillis; Parson Leavenworth owned Ped and Phillis; and Parson Scovill owned Phillis and Dick.

Aside from Africans, native Indians were also used as slaves, especially after King Philip's War. I. Woodruff, according to Bronson, owned an Indian woman who died in 1774. Even white men could end up in bondage. If a crime was severe enough, the court could sentence a white man to slavery.

Directly following the Revolutionary War, Connecticut passed an act that limited the time of servitude by slaves. No Negroes, mulattos or Indian children could be held past their twenty-fifth birthday. This same act outlined punishment for slaves wandering without a pass from their owner or the court. There was a curfew of 9:00 p.m. that had to be followed.

Without authorization, a slave would be held as a runaway. Runaways and curfew breakers were brought before the courts and could be publicly whipped.

If a white man was caught doing business with a slave past 9:00 p.m., there would be a fine.

Bronson's history was written a few years before the outbreak of the Civil War, and by then the families of slave-owning colonists had downplayed that portion of their history.

Law had curtailed slavery in 1807, mandating that no new slaves were to be imported to the United States. Since slavery was for life, propagation of new slaves was by natural means. The ban did not stop the institution.

The arguments for and against slavery were debated for the decades between the Revolutionary and Civil Wars. But the battles of the Civil War and the Emancipation Proclamation didn't end that debate. Even without an institution of slavery, the second-class-citizen status and hardships blacks faced up to and beyond the civil rights movement of the twentieth century have plagued the country.

Waterbury did not embrace the conflict of the Civil War, but it had to send men to battle. The reason why the city was not eager to participate wasn't about slavery, but about the initial reasons for the conflict—states rebellion.

But Waterbury did participate and produced a heroic figure, Colonel John L. Chatfield, who was wounded once and then reassigned to the Fifty-fourth Regiment led by Colonel Robert Shaw. In a historic battle with a historic regiment of black soldiers, Chatfield was wounded once more. He returned to his Waterbury home, where he later died.

Dr. Joseph Anderson followed Bronson's *History of Waterbury* with a three-volume saga of his own that did not mention much about slaves, except for two in particular. Caesar Rose was listed as the last freed slave in town, and he died of old age in the poorhouse. The second person mentioned was Philip Sampson, who was noted for his "size and strength." Weighing more than three hundred pounds, he could lift sixteen hundred pounds.

From the years following the Civil War until the migration north of Southern blacks, little is known, except for the institution of the AME Zion Church in town, with its 150 members, in 1896. In the South, drought, poverty and discrimination forced blacks to look elsewhere for work and a respectable life. They, like other hardworking people before them, saw the industrial North as a promised land. Waterbury, with its many factories, was not overlooked in this migration.

Jeremy Brecher's book *Brass Valley*, compiled in 1982, recounts the movement of the McDonald family. Luke McDonald's ancestors hailed from North Carolina and, like other black families, wanted a better life. They crept north, temporarily settling in Virginia, Maryland and New Jersey before landing in Waterbury. "After living in Baltimore for a while Waterbury seemed like a hick town," McDonald said.

During the summers of 1916 and 1917, McDonald worked at Scovill, while still a grammar school student. The worker shortage due to World War I encouraged black migration, and the influx of new people into town wasn't always easy. Older black residents found the newcomers rough and provincial.

Luke McDonald found work after grammar school caning chairs, working with furniture and as a bellhop at a hotel. He began work in 1927 at American Brass, where he remained for forty-one years.

The black experience wasn't unlike that of the immigrants from Europe. Men would come and find jobs before sending for their families. Blacks, however, weren't as welcome and didn't find jobs easily until immigration limited the number of Europeans entering the country. With that shift, opportunities arose, and by 1920 the city population was 1 percent black.

Aside from factory work, Waterbury offered a respite from the Ku Klux Klan.

Factory owners were faced with a grumbling workforce and strikes. Blacks were used as strikebreakers because the trade unions forbade their admittance, and therefore they were not a part of the main workforce. The need for this service didn't win blacks any perks. According to workers of the time, blacks were hauled north in cattle cars to break these strikes.

Early schools incorporated children from within walking distance. Despite the early integration, schools became more segregated. Waterbury served as the test case for desegregation, leading to the more public battle in Boston during the 1960s. *Author's collection.*

The beginnings of the unrest Waterbury faced during the civil rights era were in the early part of the century. Charles Johnson, who directed the National Urban League's Department of Research and Investigation, wrote that Negroes in Waterbury lived in close contact with one another, densely populating a few streets.

The reason for the ghetto-like conditions wasn't a desire to create a black neighborhood so much as it was a reaction to keeping other neighborhoods all white. As a result of the discrimination, black families faced higher than normal rentals. Garbage collectors routinely overlooked the streets in black neighborhoods, forcing trash to pile up throughout the winter. Lastly, Johnson reported that the city abounded with parks, but none was near Negro neighborhoods, forcing children to play in the streets.

Discrimination had become ingrained in Waterbury, as it had in many cities throughout the United States. Blacks were not becoming a part of the mainstream workforce. Black workers were assigned grunt work, and those individuals wanting to better their lot by creating their own companies were stymied by the reluctance of banks to loan them money or extend credit.

Mom and pop–type shops did exist in black neighborhoods but were limited to those neighborhoods, and their market was the population immediately around them. Larger, more successful stores drawing from this same population were white owned.

Even if thrifty black workers saved enough to buy a home of their own, the American Dream was limited to the same neighborhood where they had rented.

Conditions in the South did not improve, and people continued to move north. Factories had limited the kinds of jobs doled out to Negroes to the dirtiest, most straining chores. Construction jobs were limited to tasks like tunnel work. If a job was underpaid, dirty, exhausting and dangerous, it was a black man who filled it.

The *Waterbury Observer* compiled a history of blacks in Waterbury in 1998 and interviewed Maxine Watts. In 1997, the NAACP had wanted information about the Pearl Street Neighborhood House, and Maxine found that the Mattatuck Museum's historical archives did not contain any information about the organization. In the *Observer*, Maxine stated:

> *There was no history because of the heavy-duty segregation. We were second-class citizens whose history was not worth recording. Our community had no rapport with the newspaper and there were no reporters coming to attend any of our events.*

As a result, the museum joined with the NAACP to create an oral history project to record the memories of community elders.

As time passed in Waterbury, the few streets housing blacks expanded to two neighborhoods—Long Hill and Walnut-Orange-Walsh (WOW), with social life revolving around the Pearl Street Neighborhood House. Bowling, sewing, cooking, sports and dances were the staple. Time, however, didn't change discrimination. When heavyweight champion Joe Louis came to town, he was refused a room at the Elton Hotel on the Green. Locals felt the rub when they were refused admittance to local restaurants.

The civil rights movement began to get legs during the 1950s, and Maxine remembers going to work for Connecticut Light and Power (CL&P) in 1962. To avert an impending march on the company by the black community, it hired a token black worker. Maxine was a recent college graduate and took a placement test at the Pearl Street Neighborhood House, where the company had come to recruit that employee. She scored one hundred and got the job.

Her desk was strategically placed in the window of the Leavenworth Street office, where she was on display for the entire town to see. But getting the job was only the beginning. Co-workers had to learn that Maxine would use the restroom and eat in the lunchroom with them.

The 1960s was a watershed decade for Waterbury blacks. Dr. Martin Luther King had begun a peaceful but forthright movement for civil rights. When he was assassinated, blacks took to the streets. Images on television showed cities burning across the nation. At home, a riot broke out in the North End of Waterbury and had to be quelled by police force.

Time magazine covered the news in the summer of 1967, writing:

> *With more than 45 dead in rioting across the nation last week, thousands injured, and upwards of $1 billion in cash and property losses, Americans groped for words to fit the failure. New York's Senator Robert F. Kennedy called it "the greatest domestic crisis since the War between the States."*

The local media covered the riots in lurid detail in both newspapers and on television. Whites fled to suburbia, and the urban infrastructure began to erode. But blacks slowly began to make strides despite lingering racism. Black neighborhoods continued to be plagued with crime and drugs, and hiring remained a battlefield. Political positions were hard won, and an *Observer* editorial stated that race relations were the most explosive issue facing the United States.

The civil rights movement hit a climax with the death of Reverend Martin Luther King Jr. Waterbury, like many cities across America, erupted into violence, taxing the police and fire department to their limits. The National Guard was enlisted to bring things to rest. Waterbury Observer *Archives*.

The North End of town, where the riots occurred, never fully recovered. *Waterbury Observer Archives.*

In 1969, things did begin to change. Waterbury became the test case for desegregation, allowing the federal government to hone its skills before tackling the larger Boston school system. This move began in Topeka, Kansas, with the *Brown v. Board of Education* case of 1954. This case set the law that found that the segregation of neighborhoods was de facto discrimination. The suit forced Waterbury to desegregate its schools.

Up until then, most schools were K–8 and situated in neighborhoods. Grammar schools were within walking distance from home, and in many cases children would return home for lunch. The solution Waterbury hit on was to develop middle schools that warehoused a larger and more diverse population of students.

Maurice Mosely, city attorney for the department of education, remembered the decision. "It was enacted in the early seventies. I was in law school at the time." He recalled that Wallace was the first middle school and, in hindsight, acknowledged that the middle school solution may not have been best. "Twelve to thirteen hundred students is too large a population. It was not visionary but a solution. A better solution might have been to build better schools in neighborhoods."

As a student in the North End, his grammar school days lasted until eighth grade. As an active member in educational affairs, he could not imagine how he would have reacted to leaving the close neighborhood environment at age eleven to be warehoused with so many other children. "The noise in the halls is deafening."

Another problem was that the distance of the middle schools from many neighborhoods made it difficult for many parents to remain active in the parent-teacher organization.

CHAPTER 7

BAD BOYS

The Yom Kippur Murders

Yom Kippur fell on September 26, 1974, and Jews living in the historic Overlook District filled the local synagogues on this Day of Atonement. Following the services at Beth El Synagogue on Cook Street, attorney Irving Pasternak and his wife, Rhoda, left the ornate temple that looked out over Fulton Park, where the shadows grew long in the autumn evening. Those who knew Irving Pasternak would wonder what he had to atone for. An unpretentious man who was well liked and respected by his peers, neighbors and friends, his generosity was widely known.

It was dusk and time to break the day-long fast. Irving and Rhoda traveled a few blocks west to their daughter Myrna's on Willow Street. It was a tranquil neighborhood, and the Pasternaks' home on Fern Street was nearby. The homes in Overlook were large, gracious and inviting, many built by the brass barons who had made fortunes in Waterbury. The streets were tree-lined and cozily lit. People here knew one another and were proud of the quality of their lives. It was a night to feel blessed.

The dinner with Myrna and her family ended early, and by 9:15 p.m. Rhoda Pasternak was upstairs in her bedroom, talking on the telephone with Myrna, discussing a grandchild's upcoming bar mitzvah. Irving was downstairs in his robe, reading. When she heard the doorbell ring, Rhoda reminded her husband that it was late, admonishing him not to let anybody in.

Myrna recounted what happened next. Irving ordered someone out of his house, and there was scuffling downstairs. Rhoda was pleading with her daughter to send help. Myrna hung up the phone and dialed the police. She sent her husband over while she made one more call to her parents' neighbor.

A second call came in to the police. According to a hysterical Rhoda, a crazy man was in their house, fighting with her husband.

The crazy man was doing more than that.

When officers arrived, they expected the worst. It had been called in as a domestic dispute, the kind of call that was a crapshoot. Officers would not know what to expect—spousal abuse, child abuse or perhaps a drunken rage. But this particular call proved more horrendous than they could have imagined. The responding officers were greeted with a double homicide that would provoke the longest-running trial in Connecticut's history.

A fire extinguisher lay on the entryway floor, its spray covering a nearby wall mirror. As officers moved into the now-quiet house, they discovered Irving lying in the kitchen, dead. Rhoda was upstairs, and like her husband, had been repeatedly stabbed. The viciousness of the attack was apparent—each body had been pierced over twenty-five times.

Detectives found few clues. A bloody heel print was the most distinguishable—it bore what is known as the cat's paw design. A button and two small plastic pieces were on the floor nearby. The Pasternak home was tidy, and it seemed unlikely that Rhoda would have left debris untouched on the living room carpet.

Upstairs, the scene was equally grim. Rhoda lay sprawled, covered in blood. A six-inch buck knife lay neatly atop a pair of loafers.

Defense wounds on Irving's hands attested that he had fought his assailant. Had Rhoda called downstairs, warning the intruder that the police were on their way? Had the intruder, instead of bolting out the door, climbed to the second floor to leave no witnesses? Trapped upstairs with a madman climbing the stairs must have been excruciating for Rhoda. With nowhere to run, she may have screamed bloody murder. Yet no one outside heard a peep.

Police fanned through the neighborhood, looking for witnesses. Two women who had been out walking reported seeing a man with long hair running down the road. A young neighbor of the Pasternaks proved more fruitful. Kim Perugini did not see anything that night, but for several days before she had noticed a dark blue car with New York plates parked outside. A man was watching the Pasternak home. Her brother had worried about burglaries and wrote down the license number.

The plate came back belonging to the Pasternaks' former son-in-law. An interview with Myrna Kahan revealed that Murray Gold had indeed been in the neighborhood in the week preceding the murders. He had come to the Kahan house to visit, asking if Myrna's parents still lived on Fern Street.

This was more unusual that it seemed. The detectives learned that until that visit, Myrna and her parents had not seen Murray Gold in ten years, since his divorce from Myrna's sister Barbara. It had been a short marriage, ending in a settlement constructed by Irving.

It seemed amicable enough. Gold told police that Irving had been more than fair in distributing the assets. He had spent the decade between working first as an engineer, then as a stockbroker. He also spent time in a mental institution receiving electroshock therapy.

This was not the most notable fact about Murray's life, however. He, along with his parents and sister, was sent to Auschwitz during the Nazi regime in World War II. Before the death camps started the mass production of corpses, resistance fighters perpetrated a mass escape. The Golds fled, but not without consequences. Murray's little sister broke away from her brother's hand, fell behind and was recaptured by the Nazis. Murray and his parents had no choice but to move on, living with the guilt of that loss.

The family landed first in London, but in 1948 they relocated to the United States, where Meyer and Dina Gold built a lucrative furrier business that enabled their only living child to attend New York University. He majored in engineering. After obtaining his degree, the young man worked at Grumman Aircraft Corporation. Later, Murray had a change of career, becoming a customer's representative in the stockbrokerage house Bruns, Nordeman & Rhea in Cedarhurst, Long Island.

He had been a stocky young man, with dark eyes and hair and an olive complexion. In 1962, he met and married Barbara Pasternak, the youngest of the Pasternaks' daughters. The elder Pasternaks had no qualms about the marriage, hoping it would settle their daughter down in a comfortable life. Barbara was not of that ilk and almost balked at the wedding the night before.

It had, in hindsight, been a melting pot of two troubled spirits. Free-spirited Barbara did not want to be tied down to the staid Murray. Marriage had not settled the girl's spirit as Rhoda had hoped. In less than a year, the marriage was over. No one assigned blame, and Irving settled the assets equally between the two.

When the police looked at Murray Gold as a suspect, they did so based on his surprise visit and the fact that his car was seen near the Pasternak home. They believed that he had stalked his former in-laws for some unknown reason.

Finding that only seven months before the murders Murray had received shock treatment, the detectives began to wonder if the former son-in-law was in his right mind. Questioning him would determine how to proceed.

Murray greeted the Waterbury detectives amicably and gave his consent to have his apartment searched. During this search, the detectives found a button kit that had a button and two plastic tabs missing. They matched those found on the floor at the Pasternak home. Several sets of shoes with cat's paw heels were discovered in Murray's closet. Because these were common to many manufacturers, this find was not as telltale as the buttons, but it did add one more piece of evidence to the list. What made the detectives really sit up and take notice was that one of Murray's fingers had a deep cut that had been treated by a doctor.

Murray told them that he had injured himself cutting carrots. The building superintendent told the detectives that Murray's explanation to him was that he had cut his finger slicing potatoes. The doctor was told that the cut was the result of broken glass.

Why so many stories?

Meanwhile, in Waterbury, things had not settled down. Judge Meyers, who lived on Stephana Lane, near to the Pasternaks, reported a telephone call he had received the night of the murders. Some unknown man told him that the Pasternaks were dead and he was next. Myrna Kahan's son also reported a phone call with the threat that he and his siblings would be killed. Police guards were placed, and the investigation at home kicked into higher gear.

Since Irving Pasternak had been beloved by friends and family, some suspected what we now call a hate crime. Could the couple have been targeted simply because they were Jewish?

Governor Thomas Meskill posted a $3,000 reward for information leading to a conviction in this crime. The Waterbury Bar Association matched that amount.

A grand jury was convened, and the prosecutor laid out the circumstantial evidence. State's Attorney Francis MacDonald had hoped to tie up as many loose ends as possible, but taking a vicious killer off the streets was a priority.

The evidence before them included Kim Perugini's identification from a photo lineup of who she believed had been sitting in the car outside the Pasternak home. She chose Murray Gold. Medical records reporting the electroshock therapy, the heels of Murray's shoes, the items missing from the button case and photos of the cut finger were studied carefully. In his defense, Murray's parents swore that they were having dinner that evening, breaking the Yom Kippur fast.

Detectives had studied the timeline from when Murray left his parent's home to the trip to the emergency room for his cut finger. There wasn't much time to waste, but detectives believed that it was possible. One thing missing, however, was the lack of clothing saturated in the Pasternaks' blood. The brutal stabbings would have left the killer soaked. Could Murray have changed clothes en route or worn a coverall? So much evidence was lacking in this case.

Other suspects had been considered. The police carefully screened Irving's client lists. They looked into Barbara Pasternak's current boyfriend. He was of particular interest because he was on the FBI's most wanted list and missing. But no suspect had so clear a link to the killing as Murray.

The overriding question was why? After ten years' absence and without rancor from the past, why had the stockbroker suddenly looked up his ex-in-laws and staked out their house? Had some paranoia set in during Murray's

Murray Gold was arrested for the murders of his former in-laws, Irving and Rhoda Pasternak. *Waterbury Police Department.*

middle age? Could his reasons be beyond explanation? Had Murray always harbored a murderous heart?

Whatever the underlying reason, the grand jury had no trouble indicting Murray Gold for the murders of Irving and Rhoda Pasternak.

The Golds were distraught and hired who they believed to be the most effective lawyer for their son. William Kunsler from the Center for Constitutional Rights had gained national attention by defending the Chicago Seven, a group of young dissidents who had engineered the riots surrounding the Democratic Convention in 1968. The Golds felt that the State of Connecticut had unfairly singled out their son as a suspect in this murder because of Murray's psychiatric history. Murray had not been a bad citizen. In fact, he was a man who had never even got a parking ticket, let alone had a history of violence.

With two handsome rewards on the table, the Golds hoped that someone would step forward to clear their son's name.

Meanwhile, Kunsler accepted the challenge and began to work on a defense of reasonable doubt.

It might have been expected that he would turn to the possibilities of Barbara's boyfriend or a troubled grandchild, but William Kunsler surprised everybody by introducing the possibility of a heretofore-unknown suspect—Bruce Sanford.

Who was Bruce Sanford, and how did he emerge as a candidate for murder?

The promised rewards prompted tipsters to emerge from the woodwork. Kunsler got at least two leads that named Sanford. Unfortunately, Sanford had committed suicide, and the veracity of these tips could not be addressed with the accused. This made him, many believed, the perfect fall guy.

Bruce Sanford was a troubled man, twenty-nine years of age when he died. A self-avowed Satanist who belonged to the motorcycle gang the Peddlers of Evil, he had a long and violent history with the police department that included one shootout. He had been a habitual drug user. He also had a history of psychiatric problems and multiple attempts at suicide.

The summer before the murder, his life had taken a sudden turn. Through an acquaintance with his mother's neighbor, Robert Bourassa, he met a woman named Gloriana LaPointe. Gloriana was going through a divorce after moving with her husband to Waterbury, his hometown. With five children to care for and the financial need to return to work as a nurse, Gloriana chose Sanford as a nanny for the children, who ranged in age from eight to eighteen.

The LaPointe neighbors on Myrtle Avenue began noticing the young, denim-clad, bald man covered with tattoos. Sanford's appearance was enough to cause concern. In the early 1970s, young men were more accustomed to wear their hair shoulder length rather than shave their head completely. But the young man quietly introduced himself to the young mothers out watching their toddlers, and questions to the two younger LaPointe brothers gave some consolation that things were OK at home.

The LaPointe children, at least the four boys, had a reputation for wild behavior. While Sanford was in charge, the neighbors noticed that a routine had been set. Dinner was at five o'clock, and bedtimes and curfews were introduced. Gloriana LaPointe was a diminutive woman with a robust, New York Italian heritage and a free spirit. Eddie LaPointe was her estranged husband living around the corner from the family in his mother's apartment. A good many of the surrounding homes housed other LaPointe family members, and Gloriana felt cast adrift. She and her husband had moved to Waterbury after retiring from the armed forces. Eddie was currently employed by the city.

Gloriana's home sat perched on the corner of Myrtle Avenue and Robbins Street, directly across from the Blessed Sacrament Convent. It was a tall, two-story white house with a pitched roof large enough to house an ample attic. What made it distinctive was not that it sat perched atop a high concrete wall, but that the property contained a small red barn that was used as a garage and playroom for the children.

Inside, the home was clean and comfortable. The first floor contained a formal living room and an eat-in kitchen, family room and laundry area. The second floor housed the four bedrooms, and the attic was finished off with paneling and carpet. A tour through the house revealed that Sanford had made himself comfortable in the attic and kept his belongings tidily around the bed. What was most unique about the interior was the padlock Gloriana kept on the outside of her bedroom door. She explained that she worried that, while she worked, the kids would get into her medications and jewelry and that she also feared her ex-husband would feel free to invade her personal space while visiting the children.

The summer began uneventfully enough, with neighbors quickly getting used to Sanford minding the children. He seemed to take the responsibility seriously, knowing where the youngest two were playing and ensuring that they behaved themselves. All of the mothers noted that it seemed to be the first time that the children had someone paying attention to them, and their behavior had improved.

Gloriana LaPointe's Myrtle Avenue home, where Bruce Sanford worked as a nanny. It is here that Sanford attempted suicide on the night of the Pasternak murders. *Vicky Semrow.*

When the LaPointe divorce became final, Gloriana stunned everybody by marrying Bruce Sanford. It may have been unexpected, but not out of character for the feisty little nurse. Gloriana lived to do the unexpected. Breakfast for the kids might be a sudden, surprise picnic out of town. A room might suddenly be painted an outlandish color favored by one of the children.

The marriage seemed to please Sanford and settle him, but it infuriated the LaPointe family, who began calling social services and started legal proceedings to gain custody of the children. Gloriana reacted with the same haste in which she had entered the marriage and suddenly acquired a Haitian divorce, stating that she had to preserve her right to the children. Sanford took the divorce hard, retreating to live at his mother's and lapsing once again into a cycle of self-violence that led to his suicide.

This drama unfolding on the west side of town was connected to Irving Pasternak by the slimmest of ties. Kunsler alleged that Gloriana had approached Pasternak for legal advice. The advice she got was to divorce Sanford in order to retain custody of the children. And this advice, it was further alleged, sent Sanford into a psychotic rage strong enough to slaughter both Irving and his wife.

The initial trial began in February 1976, with Judge Robert Wall presiding. The prosecutor was Francis MacDonald, who was known to be a brilliant attorney, but whose case, this time, was based on circumstantial evidence. William Kunsler and Victor Ferrante represented the defendant, Murray Gold.

The trial today would have been the darling of Court TV. It had elements of sex, violence and danger. It had celebrity attorneys arguing in a court of law in one of the most conservative states in the country. It had a cast of characters that included some of the most prestigious members of Waterbury society, as well as some of the worst.

As the trial unfolded, Kunsler's defense of reasonable doubt took center stage. The story spun out before the jury was lurid and grotesque. In a nutshell, William Kunsler described what happened in this way: Gloriana's spurning of Sanford's love was more than the man could bear. He was again living in his mother's home on Alder Street, a place he had desperately tried to escape through marriage. His retribution, Kunsler asserted, was not aimed at the woman who turned him away but at the man who gave her the advice. Sanford went to the Pasternak home, armed with a fire extinguisher and buck knife, with the intention of killing the unsuspecting attorney.

If Kunsler's allegations were to be believed, Sanford then telephoned a judge and the Pasternak grandson to threaten their lives.

Then, after having accomplished that, Sanford was supposed to have gone to Gloriana's home, covered in blood. Gloriana drove Sanford to Waterbury Hospital, where he was treated for a superficial knife wound to the throat, before spiriting him away to Florida, where Sanford hid out until after the grand jury indicted Murray Gold. A guilty conscience forced Sanford to confess his crimes to two individuals before killing himself.

Supporting this theory were the individuals whom Sanford called. The first was an old friend, Patricia Morrison, who was what one attorney labeled a "born again Christian." She testified that a few days before the murders Sanford had called her and threatened to "get Pasternak." The night of the murders, he called Morrison again. According to this witness, Sanford pleaded with her for help, claiming that he had done a terrible thing.

Her husband Greg added, in his testimony, that in early December 1974, Sanford telephoned looking for Patricia in order to say goodbye. During their conversation, Sanford told Greg Morrison that he regretted killing Rhoda.

This testimony was followed by that of Robert Bourassa, cousin of Eddie LaPointe, and Bourassa's friend Craig Yashenko. Bourassa had initially introduced Sanford to his wife's cousin and had maintained a close relationship with Gloriana throughout her marriage to both Eddie and Bruce. They were what attorney Louis Nizer called "friends in crime and assorted malevolence." Both testified that on the night of the murders they were called to Gloriana's house at 8:00 p.m. She was worried about Sanford, who was not at home. Sanford was not found in the search they conducted. Later, they were summoned back to the house on Myrtle Avenue, where Gloriana pointed out a shirt tossed onto the landing of the cellar stairs. It was a blue denim shirt, like the kind Sanford wore, and it was covered in blood.

In December 1974, about the time Sanford was telephoning Morrison to say goodbye, he also called Bourassa to announce his intention to commit suicide. Yashenko claimed to have accompanied Bourassa on the two visits to the LaPointe home and had listened in on the December conversation through Bourassa's second phone. It was during this call that Sanford supposedly avowed that he regretted killing Rhoda.

Dr. Joel Kovel had treated Bruce Sanford the night of the murders and testified that a man came into the emergency room with a superficial cut to his throat. He further testified that he thought the amount of blood on the man (Sanford) was more than expected given the nonserious nature of the wound.

Gloriana's testimony confirmed that Sanford had indeed gone to the emergency room that night. Her recollection of the day of September 26 was that Sanford was drunk when he showed up at her home that afternoon. She took him to her bedroom, where she locked the door from the outside using the padlock she installed to secure her room. On the witness stand, Gloriana testified that she did not want her children to see Bruce drunk. Later, when she went upstairs to check on Bruce, they argued and she told him to leave. He refused and tried to cut his throat.

Gloriana, who was a nurse, immediately dressed the wound and called the police. They arrived at 10:37 p.m. and Sanford was taken by ambulance to the emergency room a block away. The next morning, she testified, she took Sanford to Florida, where he had friends. The purpose of the trip was to remove Sanford from her home and to put distance between them while Eddie sought custody of the children.

According to Gloriana, the trip south was spent with her screaming at the troubled man, telling him he was crazy and that she should simply have him institutionalized. Her impulse marriage caused more of a stir than she had expected and Sanford's unwillingness to simply disappear was more than she could stand. In Louis Nizer's book *Catspaw*, he describes their relationship as that of a demonic criminal and a subservient sexual slave, the slave being Gloriana. If one were to look at the two, that theory might hold weight—Gloriana was tiny and Sanford loomed above her.

Those who knew the two, however, would disagree. If anyone were the predator, it would be Gloriana, who was impulsive and capricious but aware of her power to arouse men. Sanford was tied to this woman, seeing her as his last port in a psychological storm. Being part of a family with a loving partner appealed to the man, and losing that chance was a substantial blow. The question remained: was the loss substantial enough for Sanford to attack a peripheral character in the drama of their lives?

The day of Sanford's suicide was painful and pitiful to hear replayed. According to Gloriana's testimony, she visited Sanford at his mother's Alder Street home. She claimed that Mrs. Sanford was drunk, passed out in her room. Bruce and Gloriana argued. Bruce sliced his wrist with a broken glass and ran, leaving a bloody trail, to his bedroom, where he locked the door. Hours passed before Gloriana managed to pry open the door. Inside the room, she noticed that Bruce had written a terse message in blood across the dresser mirror. It read, "Curse you Glory."

Gloriana knew by the look of his body that Bruce was dead. She left the home and allowed Bruce's mother to find the body.

This trial could not have been easy for the jury. On one side, you had a set of circumstantial evidence that was damning for the defendant. On the other side, the defense laid out the groundwork for another culprit. Could that cast of characters be believed?

The jury came back with the decision that they could not decide.

A second trial began on October 12, 1976, with Judge George Saden presiding. After the first trial ended, Francis MacDonald knew he had to bolster the links between Murray Gold and the evidence found at the scene. The number of witnesses for the prosecution jumped from forty-one to fifty-five.

The most notable difference between the two trials was not the number of prosecutorial witnesses, however, but the decrease in defense witnesses. Judge Saden ruled that the testimony linking Bruce Sanford to the crime was excluded. Since Sanford was deceased, everything he said was hearsay and therefore ineligible for the jury to consider.

As a result, the trial moved swiftly to the conclusion of finding Murray Gold guilty, and he was sentenced to twenty-five years to life in prison.

Gold's parents were devastated and sought help from Louis Nizer, a famous New York attorney. Nizer brought onboard some heavy hitters from his law firm and from the Waterbury area, most notably Timothy Moynihan.

Nizer approached the task with an appeal. The appeal was based on what is called the "hearsay rule." Hearsay is not allowed during a trial because the other person being quoted must be able to take the stand to be cross-examined in front of a jury. In this way, a jury can determine whether the person who did the talking is lying. In the case of Bruce Sanford, his death determined that he could never be cross-examined. Therefore, anyone could attribute any statement as having been made privately by this man without a chance of asking the source.

The appeal Nizer produced likened what Sanford had to say to that of a deathbed confession because Sanford, knowing he would kill himself, had nothing to lose. And if that were true, those testifying to what Sanford told them would have nothing to gain by the testimony. (Nizer seemed to have overlooked the prospect of reward as reason enough.)

The appeal was granted, and Murray Gold was free to go home. Time spent in prison did not agree with Murray. His behavior seemed odd to his parents and attorney—no display of glee greeted them at the prison door. Murray challenged Nizer's handling of the case, demanding a right to have participated in the appeal. No matter how much Louis Nizer explained the intricacies of the law with regard to appeal and the outcome as being favorable to his client, Murray was not assuaged.

Nizer continued to fight for his client, and before a third trial could be set he apprised the State of Connecticut that Murray had suffered in prison and had not been a danger to himself or society during the time spent on bail. Nizer feared that if paranoia had set in, Murray might not be able to fully participate in a third attempt to convict him.

According to Nizer's book, *Catspaw*, he worked out a plea bargain with the state. If Murray would plead to a lesser charge, the defendant could be sentenced to time served with the promise that he would never again enter Connecticut. The only additional condition would be that a psychiatrist of his choice treat Murray for one year.

It may have been the most favorable outcome for Murray Gold, but imagine Nizer's surprise when his client refused to consider the offer and fired the attorney who had freed him from a long prison sentence.

The third trial began with Yale professor John Williams leading the defense.

Some might wonder why the State of Connecticut would consider so generous an offer to a vicious killer if it believed Murray Gold to be responsible for the crimes. Nizer proffered several reasons.

Two witnesses recanted their testimony. Bourassa and Yashenko were charged with perjury. This strengthened the state's case, but the prosecutors realized that Gold's mental state appeared to be deteriorating. His life outside prison had been quiet and trouble free. The next trial could present Myrna Kahan's son as a possible suspect, and that would add more agony to an already troubled family. No one in Waterbury wanted to see Irving Pasternak's grandson dragged through the mud in the way Bruce Sanford had been.

By November 1984, a third trial had begun. In pretrial hearings, John Williams came out swinging. He cited that members of the jury, during the second trial when they had been sequestered, had been drinking alcoholic beverages. He further cited that defense witness George Morrison informed the defense team that the Sanford family owned a car similar to one seen at the scene of the crime. The most damning bit of information Williams imparted was aimed at the chain of evidence. It was alleged that the sewing kit taken from Murray Gold's home, the one that contained the missing button and two plastic tabs similar to those found at the scene of the crime, had actually been left unguarded and was stolen. Williams claimed that the kit being used as evidence was not, in fact, the same one taken from Murray's home.

The last thunderbolt claimed that a state trooper had altered the drawing of the crime scene to include the button. He also argued that MacDonald's remarks about Murray Gold were inflammatory.

Judge Charles Gill presided. Despite Williams's allegations, the trial was set to move forward. Problems erupted from the start of jury selection. Murray demanded more input and fought his attorney over several key selections. Soon, Murray Gold began to believe that John Williams was in cahoots with the prosecution and fired him. Judge Gill allowed Murray to represent himself, as he requested, but did not allow Williams to leave the team. He sensed that Murray Gold was in a downhill spiral and wanted to ensure that someone was watching out for Murray's rights and well-being.

The trial, in Murray's hands, became rambling, with the cross-examinations aimed at portraying Murray in a favorable light rather than deflecting the state's case. Williams chafed at the turn the trial was taking. With a case that had grown colder with every passing year, there was a chance of winning, but with Murray's meddling, things went from bad to worse.

Problems arose outside the courtroom, as well. The Holiday Inn where Murray stayed complained that he made a lot of unwarranted noise, arguing while alone. The police had been called, but no charges were filed. Murray denied making noise and felt he was being persecuted.

Judge Gill was concerned enough to order Murray to see a psychiatrist before continuing the trial. When Murray was declared incapable of proceeding, he was sent to Whiting Forensic Hospital in Middletown, Connecticut, for treatment. He was placed on drug therapy, and when the trial resumed it was clear that no progress in Murray's condition had been made.

Now a fourth trial was ordered. Before it began, it was learned that Gloriana LaPointe was put under hypnosis by investigator James Conway, who was working for William Kunsler. The session took place during the first trial, and while Gloriana was rambling and inconclusive, she did not admit that Bruce Sanford killed the Pasternaks.

The fourth trial began with Judge William Lavery presiding. Representing Murray was the team of William Collins and Nicholas Serignese from East Hartford, Connecticut. Francis MacDonald was now a judge, and Walter Scanlon took over as prosecutor. It was now ten years after the crime had been committed. This was the longest-running trial in Connecticut's history. Aside from what has been written here, the ordeal also included an exhumation of Bruce Sanford's body in which he was revealed to be wearing a shoulder-length wig that was placed on his head by his mother in an attempt to make her son more presentable in the coffin. The long wig led to finger-pointing by the defense, claiming that the long-haired runner seen by the two women on the night of the murders could have been Sanford disguised in this same manner. The exhumation, to the state's delight, showed that Sanford's shoe size did not match that of the heel print.

With hypnosis, perjured witnesses and the cast of characters involved in the attempt to cast reasonable doubt, the tragedy of the Pasternaks was often overshadowed by the circuslike atmosphere created by the witnesses. The fourth trial, so far removed from the actual crime, proved to be a more watered-down version of the first. Gloriana LaPointe had remarried three more times and was proving to be more forceful about Sanford's innocence.

It was believed by many that this would be the trial in which Murray would be acquitted, but the jury surprised them all with a guilty verdict. Murray Gold was again sentenced to twenty-five years to life in prison.

Somers Prison welcomed its newest inmate and found him to be a defeated, depressed man who suffered mentally. During the course of his imprisonment, he suffered physically, as well.

Was justice done? People in Waterbury believed it was—finally. Irving Pasternak had been beloved and was remembered for his generosity and fair play. Rhoda, who the defense always saw as an innocent victim, had been trapped and murdered by a ruthless and vicious killer. What they saw as a smoke and mirrors kind of defense had been cut through by the fourth jury, and Murray Gold would not hurt anyone again.

But, as Yogi Berra said, "It ain't over till it's over." After he had languished for years behind bars, attorneys Nizer, Kunsler, Williams, Collins, Moynihan and others involved with Gold's defense teamed up with prosecutors to put forth a great writ of habeas corpus that freed Murray Gold again.

Habeas corpus means "bring me the body." In this case, it was used as a device for a prisoner to demand a hearing to determine whether the court was illegally withholding liberty. Murray Gold had not filed any appeal after the fourth trial's conviction. The crux of this writ on Murray's behalf was that, at the time of the fourth trial, Murray was mentally incapable of defending himself. The psychiatric drugs prescribed for him made him unaware and incapable of participating in his defense.

In February 1991, more than sixteen years after the Pasternaks were brutally murdered, Murray Gold's mental state was in question, and the arguments proffered dealt with whether the diagnosis and treatment of Gold during the third and fourth trials inhibited the defendant's ability to participate. Should a trial, at that time, have been postponed to resume when Murray's mental state had improved?

On March 11, 1991, a decision was reached to grant Murray Gold a fifth trial. He never lived to see it.

Where lies the truth in this case? It was one that opened up Waterbury's various social factions for the world to see. It took place at a time when the economic strength of the city had started to crumble and the world's gaze was unwelcome. There were those who believed that Murray Gold had "snapped" for some unknown reason and focused his anger on his former in-laws. Some wanted to believe in Murray's innocence, and there was a celebrity pressure brought to bear in an attempt to assist in Murray's defense.

For those who believed Murray innocent, it was easy to point a finger at someone like Bruce Sanford, who, by all accounts, was as likable as a rabid pit bull. Those who believed in Gold's guilt had a hard time overcoming the Sanford smoke screen.

It might have been easier to try the case today. Obscure DNA evidence might have provided some conclusive proof about who was in the Pasternak house that night. But without that kind of evidence, history has to rely on facts as presented. The facts, however, do not include fingerprints, a confession or an eyewitness to the crime.

The closest we come to a witness to this crime is Rhoda Pasternak. The local paper quoted her as saying to her daughter, "A tall, young man is fighting with your father."

When she saw that man up close, was he Murray Gold?

Crane's Secret Life

Rosalind Russell was the biggest Hollywood star to emerge from Waterbury until television's Bob Crane was introduced in *Hogan's Heroes*, a sitcom based on the play and movie *Stalag 17*.

Crane played the lead and imbued the character of Colonel Hogan with a mischievous, wholesome quality that the audiences loved. It was a popular, award-winning show that earned its star face recognition everywhere.

Bob Crane was born in Waterbury in July 1928 and began playing drums professionally while still a teen. He dropped out of high school and spent a year drumming for the Connecticut Symphony before launching a career as a dance band drummer. In 1949, he married his high school sweetheart,

Ann Terzian, and together they had three children, Deborah Ann, Karen Leslie and Robert David.

Crane spent the early years of his career following the drumming phase as a disc jockey. When his popularity grew to a level where it threatened the ratings of another station, he was lured away by CBS in 1956 and relocated to Los Angeles, where he became known as the "king of the Los Angeles airwaves."

As his success mounted, neighbors in the Robinwood section of Waterbury lauded Crane as a good family man who visited his parents, Alfred and Rosemary Crane, as well as his brother Al. Everyone knew when he came to town because he could be seen at Blessed Sacrament Church with them on Sunday morning.

As a disc jockey in Tinsel Town, Crane interviewed legendary stars and used his quick wit to keep the show lively and fresh. Always eager to try new things, Crane began appearing on television, subbing for Johnny Carson's daytime show *Who Do You Trust?* and appearing on the *Twilight Zone*, *The Lucy Show*, *Alfred Hitchcock Presents*, the *G.E. Theater* and *The Dick Van Dyke Show*. He also had a recurring role on *The Donna Reed Show*.

With each appearance, Crane honed his acting skills, and the audiences responded to his handsome guy-next-door manner. He was the kind of guy that viewers could picture livening up a dreary party, a blast to be with on the golf course and a modern family man. He had charisma.

That's why in 1965 it was no surprise when he was cast in a leading role on nighttime television. The show *Hogan's Heroes* was set in a Nazi POW camp where the prisoners were in charge, though the Nazis didn't know it. Hogan was the kind of leader the men respected, and he was offbeat enough to come up with outlandish schemes to fulfill their missions under the Nazis' noses. Despite some initial reactions to making a comedy of so serious a subject, the show was immensely popular and ran from 1965 to 1971.

During this run, Crane received two Emmy nominations, appeared in a movie—*The Wicked Dreams of Paula Schultz*—with Swedish bombshell Elke Sommer and posed on the cover of *TV Guide* twice.

Toward the end of the show's run, Bob Crane surprised fans by divorcing his wife of twenty years and marrying Patricia Olsen, who, under the stage name of Sigrid Valdis, played Hilda, the sexy camp secretary.

Disney cast Crane in two films following the demise of *Hogan's Heroes*. *Super Dad* and *Gus* paid the bills, as did appearances on *Police Woman*, *Quincy ME* and *The Love Boat*. Finally, in 1975 he was offered his own show on NBC. *The Bob Crane Show* lasted a mere three months.

Despite Crane's continued wholesome image, there was a dark side to the actor that wasn't revealed until his untimely death in 1978.

It began with an introduction by Crane's costar Richard Dawson to a video enthusiast named John Carpenter. Carpenter, Dawson explained, was an electronics expert who sold VCRs and was a photography aficionado just like Crane.

The friendship blossomed, and their mutual interests were explored. After Crane's death, the seedy details emerged.

Crane and Carpenter would trawl for women. This wasn't hard given Crane's good looks and fame. The two would videotape themselves and the women enjoying group sexual encounters. Crane's appetite seemed insatiable.

In 1978, while Bob Crane was appearing in Scottsdale, Arizona, the friendship soured, and Crane suddenly severed ties with Carpenter. The next day, Bob Crane was found bludgeoned to death in a hotel room. No weapon was found at the Winfield Place Apartments, though a camera tripod was missing. The news first leaked that, while doing a play called *Beginner's Luck*, Bob Crane had been brutally slain by persons unknown.

Though he was a favorite suspect, Carpenter was not charged with the crime.

In 1992, the cold case was reopened, and as a result John Carpenter was finally arrested and tried in 1994. The trial showed footage of the two men in orgies and having sex with the same woman. A close bond between the victim and the defendant was proven, but not enough solid evidence linked Carpenter to the crime and he was acquitted. Carpenter died in 1998.

The lurid details exposed by the trial led Hollywood filmmakers to producing *Auto Focus*, a biography of Crane's life and murder. It depicted the former star as a churchgoing family man until his remarriage to Olsen. Then, according to the film, Crane became a sex addict.

Olsen and their son, Robert Scott Crane, objected to the portrayal, saying that the tendencies Crane had toward the lurid had been a part of the man long before *Hogan's Heroes*.

His fans were stunned by the revelations. Having been known as a wholesome family man and a politically conservative celebrity, the image of Bob Crane as a seedy sexual predator was disappointing.

The Purolator Massacre

As the police reconstructed the crime: It was a dark night on April 16, 1974. Rain clouds obscured the starlight, making the conditions perfect for the two couples sneaking through the Yellow Cab parking lot on Store Avenue. They crept along, watchful of lights going on in the nearby apartments, listening for any door to open lest they be caught. Time moved slowly until they reached the chain-link fence separating the cab parking lot from the back driveway of the old post office garage.

Quietly, they cut the fence links to create a space large enough for each to slip through into the adjacent driveway.

Inside the Yellow Cab dispatch office, Rose Thierault was working her first night on the job dispatching cabs to various locations throughout Waterbury. She had no idea that there were people in the lot outside her door.

At 4:00 a.m., an armored car pulled into the garage lot. The drop off of the Hartford area pick-ups for the Purolator company was on time. Inside the cab of the truck sat William West, fifty, and Edward Cody, forty-six. West had worked for Purolator for the past five years; Cody was a veteran Hartford police officer moonlighting for extra money. Both men were experienced, especially Cody, who had twenty-five years in law enforcement.

The men may have sighed their relief at reaching the garage. Most robberies occurred en route. Reaching Waterbury meant that they could let down their guard, especially once the garage door closed behind them. Now it was time to unload the truck so that another set of drivers could pick up the contents.

As the unalarmed door slid shut, the two couples quietly crept forward.

The attack was quick. A cinderblock thrown through the garage door window allowed access for the high-powered rifles that blasted thirty to sixty rounds of bullets inside, killing the two men instantly. Cody was still in his seat when the bullets flew through the open truck door that faced the broken window. West fell in front of the truck. West had been a deacon in the First Congregational Church in Cromwell. Neither man had time to draw the .38 pistols they carried on their belts.

With the guards down, the couples went to work quickly. A wooden panel in the door was kicked in and the four slithered inside, gathering the $1.8 million in cash, checks, food stamps and jewelry bundled in bags. The robbers did not venture in too far, settling for the loot at hand. Had they turned a corner, another $2 million would have been theirs for the taking.

The Yellow Cab Company parking lot provided a clandestine portal to the Purolator driveway. *Vicky Semrow.*

Rose Thierault didn't hear a thing. None of the tenants in the apartments near the depot reported a disturbance. The couples had come and gone without notice.

The crime scene wasn't discovered until James Fagas, a Purolator employee, reported for work at 7:30 a.m. He called the police, who brought in the FBI to help with the investigation.

At first, the detectives feared it had been an inside job. Leslie Clark, thirty-eight, was supposed to have been stationed in the garage that shift and he was missing. Clark had worked for the company for eight years, but financial downturns and personal problems could change a loyal employee's ethics.

Mayor Edward (Mike) Bergin joined the scene, which one detective described to the reporters as "a blood bath." John Griffin was the chief inspector.

It wasn't until the crime scene investigators lifted a fallen telephone booth that the body of Clark was found. Suddenly, it wasn't an inside job and the clues got smaller.

The four robbers emerged from behind the Yellow Cab Company to sneak up on the Purolator garage. The Yellow Cab building is on the left. Directly behind the parking lot is the Franco American Club. *Vicky Semrow.*

It was determined that approximately $900,000 in cash and $66,000 in jewelry was missing from the depot, making it the largest robbery in Connecticut.

Rewards were offered. Governor Ella Grasso put up $60,000 for tips leading to the arrest of the culprits. It was hoped that the high reward meant that the brazen armed invasion would not go unsolved.

The police used the media to ask the public for help. And help arrived.

Tips came in, with one caller whispering the name, "Pelletier."

A photograph of a known criminal named Lawrence Pelletier was shown on television and a Meriden gun dealer called the police. He reported that he had sold two M1 high-powered rifles, describing how a man fitting Pelletier's description came in and filled out the required forms to purchase the guns. A woman claiming to be his wife came in later to pay for the guns.

A license wasn't required at the time, and the sale was legal.

On April 18, the headlines in Waterbury reported that the robbers had been captured and the death penalty would be sought.

The four arrested were Lawrence Pelletier, thirty-six; his live-in girlfriend Evelyn Vega, twenty-six; Donald Couture, twenty-six; and his wife Donna Couture, twenty-three. The police took no chances in the capture of what they believed to be cold-blooded killers. When the time came to make the arrests at Pelletier's Carmen Street apartment, the streets were sealed and a large squad of officers moved in, prepared for trouble. Pelletier and Vega were taken from their apartment quietly at 1:15 a.m.

In Wallingford, the Coutures were also apprehended quietly, though police reported having to pull Donald out from a hiding place under the bed.

During the arrests, the police discovered more rifles, drugs, wire cutters and cash.

Pelletier was clearly the leader. He was the oldest and had a criminal career that started after he dropped out of high school. Former teachers remembered him as smart but "no stranger to trouble." His nickname from the time when he grew up on Garrigus Court in Wolcott was "Buddy." While on parole from Somers State Prison, Pelletier was caught breaking into Drug City in Watertown, Connecticut. He also tried to break into a Cheshire pharmacy.

At that time, the police believed there might still be others who participated in the crime.

The four were charged with capital murder. Police Superintendent Frederick Sullivan called the crime a "senseless slaughter." A crowd of two hundred milled about the front of the courthouse, waiting to see the perpetrators brought to justice.

Lawrence Pelletier was the eldest of the gang and had a serious criminal record. *Waterbury Police Department.*

Evelyn was Lawrence's common-law wife and would later accept a plea deal in exchange for her testimony. *Waterbury Police Department.*

Donald Couture tried to hide when police raided his home. *Waterbury Police Department.*

Donna Couture, like Evelyn, accepted a plea agreement in exchange for her testimony. *Waterbury Police Department.*

They appeared harmless enough; no haughty bravado gave the crowd any clue to the true nature of these people, who, before that day, could have blended into any crowd in any town in Connecticut. Donald Couture was dragged before the judge shoeless.

Inside, the defendants were under scrutiny. The presiding judge immediately demanded that Couture receive shoes. He then got to know more about the people standing before him. The two women had no previous arrests. Donald Couture had been working until the previous summer delivering soft drinks and, before that, furniture.

Pelletier was well known to the police as a thief who was mixed up with drugs, a growing scourge in town. He was tall and husky with curly gray hair. His rap sheet contained convictions for robbery and possession of weapons.

In 1970, the two men now standing before the bench had attempted to rob Quinlan's Home Center in Meriden, and so a past relationship was quickly established.

Donna Couture was the mother of two children. One still resided with her.

Each defendant was placed under a $750,000 bond.

In early June, the two women were brought before the grand jury to reduce their charges to $50,000 apiece. One newspaper reported that the women were claiming not to have been at the scene of the robbery and murders, and they had cooperated with the grand jury.

Evelyn Vega's testimony during the grand jury hearing included her attempt to prevent murder, according to the newspapers. She said that at one point she acquired two-inch surgical tape and practiced using it as a gag on Pelletier. The tape proved too weak to keep his mouth closed and the idea was abandoned.

Each was warned not to leave the state and to have no contact with the men or their agents.

Donna Couture went home to Ward Street in Wallingford with her parents, and Evelyn Vega was sent to her mother's home on Short Beach in New Haven.

As the first steps toward trial were taken, the security industry assessed itself. With most armored car robberies happening on the road, this assault called attention to stricter practices in depots. The assault in Waterbury happened because the only thing between the money and robbers was a garage door with a window. Alarming the door wasn't enough. The alarm was turned off to enable the car to enter, and the robbers worked swiftly enough to ensure that none of the guards within was able to reactivate the alarm or to trigger a call to the police.

Most of the security specialists studying this assault and robbery believed that there was no intention of asking the guards to hand over their bags. The firearms used in the attack were serious and outgunned the pistols issued to Purolator guards. A surprise attack on the street with that kind of firepower would have been sufficient to rob the truck. This, they felt, was a planned affair that would leave no witnesses.

The insurance executives looking at the case called a wooden garage door and a chain-link fence "dumb precautions," and every company scrambled to upgrade its own security.

On the first day of summer, public defenders Raymond Quinn and Louis Avitable objected to Judge Walter Pickett reducing the bonds of the women and the order refusing contact with the men's defense team. Quinn claimed that the order had a "chilling effect" on preparing the case for Pelletier's trial.

Prosecutor Francis MacDonald said the ban was neither against the attorneys nor their investigators.

Pelletier's response to the ban was to launch a hunger strike to protest the loss of his wife's communication. Throughout the summer, Pelletier's weight dropped fifty pounds. On September 10, 1979, the reason for the hunger strike became clear. The story read in the papers like a detective thriller.

That night, Pelletier summoned a guard to his cell at 10:30 p.m. He wanted to do his laundry. The guard escorted the prisoner to the laundry/shower room in the New Haven Correctional Center's hospital. Once there, he managed to break into a locked room called "the chase." In the chase was a trapdoor below the sink, where Pelletier broke through and, carrying a blanket, squeezed into a vertical air duct that measured ten by fifteen inches. At six feet, four inches and still weighing over two hundred pounds, he was a tight fit.

Using the blanket draped over an overhead pipe to carry his weight, Pelletier made his way through the suspended ceiling and over a wall that separated the chase from the lobby.

Guard Ellen Flagg was on lobby duty and from behind her plastic partition the sudden drop of a dangerous prisoner from above the ceiling surprised her. She told the papers that it was a "petrifying sight."

The alarm was sounded, and guards chased the escapee up Whalley Avenue until they lost the trail at a busy intersection.

Jail warden Francis Moore notified law enforcement, and the media began showing pictures of Pelletier on the television. Better security measures were put in place in the inner city jail housing four hundred.

Evelyn Vega and Donna Couture were scheduled to appear at court in Waterbury the following morning. With Pelletier loose, extra police were assigned to cover the courthouse. All parties agreed that morning that the women's appearance should be rescheduled. Donna Couture changed her representation by Hugh Keefe and was with her new attorney, Michael Graham of Hartford. Vega was with New Haven attorney David Rosen. She was whisked away with extra guards to a secure location. Pelletier was a stone-cold killer as far as law enforcement was concerned, and disposing of a witness was not beyond his capabilities. Why else would he break out? Was he sending Vega a message?

Pelletier had made his way to Waterbury by walking to Woodbridge, where he stole a new tan Ford. Somewhere between Woodbridge and Waterbury, Pelletier managed to change his clothing from the brown shirt and pants issued in jail to a black shirt and jeans. He also shaved his beard.

While the state was in an uproar trying to locate the missing prisoner, Pelletier calmly walked into the Trepid Fox strip bar in Waterbury. The Chase Avenue club featured exotic dancers and a dimly lit bar. Patrons of the place noticed the resemblance to the photo on the television and began to take bets whether the new guy was Pelletier or not. The odds were twenty to one.

Several hours were spent drinking mixed drinks before Pelletier embarked on a couple of games of setback, settling into a corner table with three other men. He introduced himself as "Bud." Bud and his partner won the first hand but lost the second.

Suspicions about Pelletier's identity were finally satisfied when he introduced himself by his rightful name to one of the dancers.

A tip came in to Officer Louis Palermo, and the call went out over the police radio. Detectives Robert Little and Thomas Brown were in their unmarked car, and they responded. They were at the Trepid Fox within minutes. Sixteen other officers surrounded the place. It was 6:30 p.m. when Detective Little walked in and Pelletier bolted toward the backroom, where the go-go dancers performed, and into a room near the kitchen. Thomas Brown was outside the padlocked door, and he kicked it in. His gun was drawn, and he pointed it at Pelletier. "If you move, it's all over," Brown warned.

A minor scuffle ensued but was quelled by the arrival of Detective Little and Sam Beamon, who handcuffed the captured prisoner.

Out in the bar, the patrons were explaining to the arriving officers that they had been too afraid to report Pelletier's presence. Later, after Pelletier was carted away, the bar patrons tried to sell off the stolen Ford for twenty-five dollars.

Pelletier refused to talk to the police.

In this case, history repeated itself. When Pelletier was in custody in 1965, he claimed to be suicidal and was taken to Norwich Hospital, where he escaped.

The police and court system considered Pelletier one of its most dangerous criminals, and his powers of persuasion were not overlooked. That is why a no-contact order was made for the two women. Pelletier was not jailed with Couture, who was in custody in Hartford.

When notable trial lawyer John Williams was asked his thoughts regarding Pelletier's escape, he told the *Waterbury Republican-American*:

> *This is just the latest episode in the tragic saga brought about by the vicious behavior of the prosecuting authorities and the judicial authorities of the state. No person, however well put together psychologically, could have survived the brutal and inhuman pressures put upon this man by the prosecution and judges. They are seeking not only to execute him but seeking to have that execution performed by the woman he most loved and denying him the right to speak to her, even to see her, during the long period of confinement effectively on death row.*

In short, he saw the escape as predictable.

The people of Waterbury and the prosecution differed from Williams's sentiment. The only vicious people they recognized were the stone-cold killers who took the lives of hardworking fathers and husbands. Pelletier and the others were arrested because they chose to steal and chose to kill. Pelletier's psychological angst was not considered equal in loss. The people of Waterbury had their fill of violent crime.

The trial came in 1981, and Evelyn Vega waived her Fifth Amendment rights and agreed not to claim spousal privilege, though as a woman not legally married to Pelletier in a state without common law provisions she did not have that recourse. In return for leniency, she agreed to testify for the state and had her trial separated from the others. She was now represented by Robert Axelrod of Meriden.

Her trial consisted of reading this agreement aloud before Judge T. Clark Hull. Still claiming to be an accomplice only, her attorney said of Evelyn:

Nevertheless, she has come to believe that even the minor and comparatively innocent role she may have played would lead ultimately to her conviction; not because of actual guilt on her part but because of her association with the two perpetrators and the technical guilt which may have resulted.

The two women were sentenced in 1984 to thirteen years to life imprisonment.

The men were viewed with a colder eye. The prosecutor, Walter Scanlon, let the jury know that he believed them to be cold-blooded killers without conscience or morals. His was vociferous in his attacks on their characters and won convictions that sentenced each man to twenty-five years to life for each man killed. The convictions would run consecutively, meaning the minimum time served was seventy-five years.

In 1985, the Connecticut Supreme Court overturned the murder conviction of Lawrence Pelletier on the grounds of MacDonald's descriptions. He, along with Couture, was granted a new trial.

Scanlon's descriptions included calling the two men "rats, murderous fiends, machine gun macho, utterly merciless killers." In a four-to-one decision, the higher court found that those remarks might have tainted the jury's perception.

Aside from causing more stringent methods of protection for armored car personnel and depots, laws were also affected. State Representative William Scully of Waterbury reacted to the deadly robbery by introducing legislation that made multiple murders a capital offense in Connecticut.

At the time, the Purolator robbery was the second-largest robbery in the country. The only one to top it was the Lufthansa Cargo Terminal robbery at JFK International Airport in New York.

Fyodor's Deportment

Fyodor Federenko sat in a New Haven court in 1981 and admitted to being a Nazi death camp guard at the Polish camp Treblinka. How he entered the United States following World War II and worked an entire twenty-three-year career at Scovill in Waterbury was a question the United States government wanted answered.

Immigrants coming to the United States in the postwar years were required to fill out paperwork that listed their occupations during the war. Federenko claimed to have been a Polish farmer who was deported to Germany to

Scovill, as well as other brass factories, sprawled throughout town. Fyodor Federenko spent a career here working before retiring to Florida. *Author's collection.*

work in the factories. The seventy-four-year-old man who had been living in retirement in Florida said that the paperwork was already filled out for him in 1949, when he asked to come to America.

Using a Russian interpreter, Federenko was asked why he lied about his wartime status. The old man answered that he "simply wasn't asked." As for the false information he could read on the paper, why had he allowed a lie to stand? Federenko explained to the court that his intent was to change the information once he landed on American soil. He blamed U.S. official Ralph Clark for falsifying the papers Federenko had used to enter the country.

In January, he was stripped of his citizenship when the deportation hearing started, and in May Federenko handed in his passport and naturalization papers.

Judge Gordon Sachs of the U.S. Immigration and Naturalization Services asked the prisoner to explain how he came to be a Nazi war criminal. Federenko explained that he had been forced by the Nazis to serve as a prison guard. Then, in 1943, there had been an uprising at the camp, and shots were fired over the heads of Jews as they fled toward freedom.

At that time, he continued, Jews were firing back at the guards and so the gunfire continued. He was, he insisted, under direct supervision at all times by the German commander—not firing at the prisoners was never an option.

Treblinka was a Nazi death camp in Poland set up to exterminate Jews. Hundreds of thousands died and were cremated in the unceasing fires of the ovens.

U.S. attorney Joseph Lynch of the U.S. Justice Department's Office of Special Investigations asked if Federenko knew that Jews were brought to the camp to be killed. Federenko answered, "We were not told what was going to happen, but unofficially we knew and the Jewish people knew what was happening."

In Florida, where Federenko had been living since his retirement in 1974, the judge hearing this case said that there was no evidence that he had committed any atrocities. But, he stated, there is enough evidence concerning the omissions on the immigration papers to revoke citizenship.

That decision was overturned on appeal and backed by the United States Supreme Court.

In Connecticut, where the deportation trial was held, Federenko faced eleven allegations, of which four points of law being approved would result in deportation. Federenko opted to be sent to the Soviet Union, where he had family, when he learned that the decision would not go his way.

New Haven attorney Brian Gildea, who defended Federenko, applied to the Soviet Union for voluntary immigration. Federenko told the court that he preferred to remain in America but that his wife and child were now living in the Ukraine. If he had to emigrate, that would be his preference.

The government's decision to prosecute this potential war criminal was backed by President Ronald Reagan and lauded by the Simon Wiesenthal Center, whose mission was to hunt down war criminals in order to bring them to justice.

When he arrived in the Soviet Union, Federenko was tried and convicted for treason and mass murder while serving the Nazi government. Fyodor Federenko, the former Scovill worker, was the first person extradited from the United States to the Soviet Union. His sentence was death by hanging, carried out on July 27, 1987.

BIBLIOGRAPHY

Anderson, Joseph. *The History of Waterbury*. New Haven, CT: Price and Lee Co., 1896.

Brecher, Jeremy, Jerry Lombardi, Jan Stackhouse and Brass Workers History Project. *Brass Valley*. Philadelphia: Temple University Press, 1982.

Bronson, Henry. *The History of Waterbury*. Waterbury, CT: Bronson Bros., 1858.

Garrow, David J. *Liberty and Sexuality*. New York: Macmillan, 1994.

Hartford Courant

Mullner, Ross. *Deadly Glow*. American Public Health Association, 1999.

Nizer, Louis. *Catspaw*. New York: Carroll & Graf Publishers, 1992.

Pape, William. *The History of Waterbury and the Naugatuck Valley*. Chicago: S.J. Clark Publishing, 1918.

Van Cleve, Jane. Oral History of Michele Russo. Smithsonian Archives of American Art, 1983.

Waterbury Observer

Waterbury Republican-American

ABOUT THE AUTHORS

Edith Reynolds grew up on the shore of New Haven Harbor and moved to Waterbury nearly forty years ago. She currently owns and operates the John Bale Book Company and Café with her husband, Dan Gaeta. With their two girls, Helen and Sarah, grown, Edith and Dan have served as urban pioneers, purchasing a building to house their antiquarian bookstore and converting the fourth floor into a loft living space.

As a former educator, college administrator and reporter, Edith has a love for history and community growth. She currently serves the city as a board member for Main Street Waterbury, the Downtown Business Association, the Mayor's Economic Task Force and the Waterbury Development Corp. She also serves on the grants boards for the Connecticut Community Foundation and for the WDC HUD block grant disbursements.

Her last book was a history of Savin Rock in West Haven, Connecticut.

John Murray began his independent community newspaper sixteen years ago in Waterbury after a career as a photojournalist at a larger newspaper. The *Waterbury Observer* is a free monthly publication that has grown into a powerhouse for information, with Murray tackling touchy, important subjects like worker health, civil rights, political corruption and, most currently, the search for a missing young man.

His in-depth coverage has earned him national acclaim that he shares with his daughter, Chelsea. Together they have brought the city another source of news.

A long-standing history of naval service in the Murray family is evident in John and Chelsea. Both have traveled the globe, bringing home stories of Asia, South America, Europe and various parts of America.